CAUDILLO

Guzman-Blanco

CAUDILLO

A PORTRAIT OF
ANTONIO GUZMÁN BLANCO

BY GEORGE S. WISE

GREENWOOD PRESS, PUBLISHERS
WESTPORT, CONNECTICUT

PREFACE

Dr. GEORGE S. WISE, who is not only a discerning student of historical and contemporary social phenomena, but also a man of vigorous activity in practical undertakings as well, has made a valiant incursion into Venezuelan history in search of the caudillo.

There have been many caudillos in the history of Venezuela, as in the history of all Latin America. The nineteenth century is the period during which creole caudillos flourished —a species of political saurian doomed to extinction by the change in the economic, social, and cultural environment. Their names still resound with the accent of a fearful magic: Rosas, Francia, Melgarejo, Don Porfirio, Lilith, Estrada Cabrera. There is great variety among them: some are military men who spring from civil war encampments; others are civilians—men who use the word instead of the sword, but often as violently; some are expansive and vigorous; others are cold, calculating politicians. But evident in all are certain common traits which allow the identification and study of the genre.

All the Venezuelan caudillos emerge from war. The first rises from the royalist ranks at the time of the struggle for independence. He is Boves, a man of numerous peculiarities and a Spaniard rather than a Venezuelan. Later come Páez, Monagas, Falcón, Guzmán Blanco, Crespo, Castro, and Gómez. From among all of them Dr. Wise has chosen Guzmán Blanco.

He tells us that his subject is not one of the most characteristic and outstanding examples of the category. He is a man in whom a variety of the features of the caudillo phenomenon is combined in a kind of reflexive moderation. He

is primarily an academic civilian who, to further personal
plans, becomes a militarist. He is a man of culture, enam-
ored of some liberal ideas, whose action reflects an obvious
wish to contribute to the nation's progress. His hardness is
calculated and his cruelty more ostentatious than effective.
Along with his greed appears his undeniable ability as an
administrator. All this makes his personality more complex
and analysis of it more difficult.

It is an arduous task to form an objective picture of this
personage. His lot is cast as a partisan in a flaming atmosphere of passion and violence. Almost everything written
about him in life was either diatribe or eulogy. For his
political friends there were never enough adjectives to use
in his praise. His adversaries found all deprecations too mild
to affront him strongly enough.

Dr. Wise, with his vivid human interest in Latin American affairs and with the prudence and sureness of method
of the man of science, has succeeded in giving us an objective view of the man who serves admirably as an introduction to and presentation of the caudillo phenomenon.

Dr. Wise has many advantages for this objective evalua-
tion. He is a man regarding a historical fact from without,
free of inherited passions or of engaged interests. He is withdrawn from the attitude of the romantic historians, who
hurled imprecations at the caudillo in the name of scorned
liberty, and he is also withdrawn from the no less dangerous
attitude of the creole positivists, who tried to justify the fact
of caudillismo and make it acceptable in the name of European theories.

Dr. Wise sees the caudillo emerge at a determined time
and within a frame of similarly determined social and economic circumstances—in a historical pattern characterized
by the existence of conflicting social groups and strata and
by the absence of a sufficiently well established institutional

structure. One would also have to add the influence of an old colonial tradition of three centuries of absolute authority and nonrepresentative government.

Under such conditions it would necessarily follow that the stability and strength of the democratic institutions which the more cultured portions of the population heroically and persistently sought to found would be precarious. In this struggle, which Sarmiento was to call that of civilization and of barbarism and which is nothing more than that between tradition and new ideals, the caudillo, who personified much of the tradition, was frequently to gain the victory.

Dr. Wise discovers these conditions and characteristics and makes them manifest in Guzmán Blanco's activity. He works in a medium that faithfully brings out some of the most important traits of the caudillo phenomenon. This is not the case of the theorist who imagines a theory and tries to illustrate it with examples, but exactly the opposite—the case of the scientific writer who analyzes an actuality. From this analysis stem elements and information which can then be used in formulating a theory.

When the time comes for a definitive theory of the creole caudillo, which is still debatable material, it is unquestionable that this work by Dr. Wise will constitute one of the most important bases on which that theory will be founded.

ARTURO USLAR-PIETRI

Caracas, 1951

Foreword

THE HISTORICAL PATTERN of Latin American countries in the nineteenth century, despite great variations in some respects, exhibited certain underlying similarities. For a quarter of a century there were wars of independence in nearly all of the Spanish-speaking countries, and during the remainder of the century almost every one of the new nations was preoccupied with organizing itself into a political and economic unit. In this task of attaining national unity the countries were subject to rather similar conditions. They had a colonial heritage which had restricted and channeled their economic development and had given them little scope for the exercise of their own political capacities; a class structure based largely on colonial domination and racial diversity; and an Iberian culture that gave great scope to Catholicism, to landed aristocracy, and to semifeudal institutions. Furthermore, certain underlying conditions were broadly characteristic of the Latin American terrain as a whole.

It is not surprising, then, that in the evolution of their political behavior a common pattern or tendency should emerge, overriding to a considerable extent the differences of various kinds that distinguished one country from another. This common or frequent manifestation of political behavior in Latin America we have chosen to designate as caudillismo, and our main task is, within limits, to delineate its nature and to throw light on its existence.

Wherever the people are inert, class-bound, sunk in poverty, and illiterate, they are ruled by constitutional oligarchies headed by a chief, by a king, or by an emperor. Unity and order are sustained by tradition and authority, back of which lies the economic and political dominance of the ruling class. Where, on the other hand, the people have democratic aspirations but are disunited, distracted by the deeper cleavages of racial or of religious or of political ideology, there the stage is set for the dictator. Our age has had and still has experience aplenty of this new portent. But there is another kind of dictator who belongs somewhere between the old dynast and the new ideological ruler. The conditions from which he springs are partly those of the older world and partly those of the newer. He is not the product of ideological clash, the bitter war of opposite faiths. He arises where the democratic aspirations of the modern world are stirring but where these are balked by the inertness and the poverty and the lack of training of the people, by the insulation that holds localities and regions apart, and by the dividing lines between the diverse racial elements of the population. This is the dictator, Latin American style—the caudillo.

He is a very different character from the dictator, modern European style. He plays a very different role. Rather little attention has been given to his historical significance. He is, so to speak, the receiver of the bankrupt colonial regime of Latin America. In a few of these countries his function has already been fulfilled.

Caudillismo is a form of dictatorial rule that can be clearly differentiated from other types of dictatorship. It is a particular species of a much larger genus. As such, it has characterized a relatively short period of modern history. Hence, it is not unreasonable to enquire whence it sprang, why it evolved, and why it assumed its special features. Historians and students of politics have offered their explanations. There is, however, room for a more intensive study devoted directly to this phenomenon. It is always easy to say that a historical phenomenon is the result of a total situation, but that blank form of statement tells us nothing. What is significant is to trace the relevance of the conditions so that their rapport with the phenomenon itself will emerge clearly. We cannot expect to give anything like a complete answer to this question, but we hope at least, within the limits of our method, to give intimations and evidences that will make the phenomenon more understandable.

There have been very many caudillos in Latin America. They have been of all kinds. We shall take one out of the many—a case study of the caudillo. However he may differ from some others, his way of rule is characteristic, his response to conditions is true to form. We take one man and one country. The country is Venezuela, the man, Antonio Guzmán Blanco. We shall see that the various aspects of his rule and the conditions under which he ruled are integrally bound together. Had some other particular caudillo been chosen, the story would have been quite different in many respects. Nevertheless, there are certain features in the rule of this caudillo that manifested themselves again and again in the history of other Latin American countries, and by a detailed analysis of his career we get a more intimate picture of the mechanisms involved than could have been attained by a broad comparative analysis of all or many caudillo regimes in Latin America.

The choice of Venezuela as the locale and of Guzmán Blanco as the special subject of our study was dictated partly by the writer's personal acquaintance with the country and partly by the conviction, based on some knowledge of several different Latin American nations, that here were encountered the features of caudillismo in a sort of average sense rather than in an extreme sense. Venezuela does not manifest all of the peculiarities that countries such as Paraguay, Ecuador, and Guatemala exhibit, and yet it does not closely resemble countries at the opposite extreme, such as Chile and Argentina. It is Caribbean and yet Continental, racially mixed and yet neither an Indian nor a Negro country. It is medium in area, population, and economic development. In turn, Guzmán Blanco was not so extreme a tyrant or so benevolent a president as could be found. The reader will note that in many respects he was a comparatively modest example of his species, although the essential traits were virtually all there.

ACKNOWLEDGMENTS

THE INVESTIGATIONS WHICH LED to the writing of this book extended over several years in many Latin American countries where the writer met with the fullest cooperation of prominent scholars too numerous to be listed here. It is a pleasure, however, to record his obligation to Dr. Arturo Uslar Pietri and Mr. Rafael Ángel Rondón Márquez of Venezuela. The writer is especially grateful to Professor Robert M. MacIver of Columbia University, whose friendship of many years and whose guidance helped to overcome difficult periods of doubt and hesitation, and to Professor Kingsley Davis of Columbia University for his invaluable advice in the final stages of the preparation of this work. Above all, the writer is indebted to his wife whose encouragement and forebearance made this book possible.

G. S. W.

Contents

ILLUSTRATIONS

CHAPTER I

RACES AND CLASSES
IN COLONIAL VENEZUELA

IN ORDER TO UNDERSTAND THE CONDITIONS which made possible the rise and the rule of a man like Guzmán Blanco, it is necessary to understand the social conditions of the country over which he ruled. As we survey these conditions historically two characteristics are outstanding. The first is the diversity of groups and strata; the second, the lack of an institutional structure sufficiently well established and accepted to prevent this diversity of groups and strata from resulting in cleavage and disruption—in other words, of any means by which the loyalties of different groups could be combined in an overall loyalty.

The Spanish colonial policies were not of such a character that they could overcome the divisiveness within Venezuelan society, but rather in certain instances they tended to take advantage of the divisiveness to foster it.

It is not enough, however, to note what is seemingly an outstanding fact about Venezuelan social organization. From our point of view it is also necessary to raise the question of whether this divisiveness has anything to do with the subsequent rise of a caudillo regime such as that of Guzmán Blanco.

The lesson of history and the logic of society alike give the answer, yes. Wherever ethnic or racial or cultural divisions are deep and unbridged, no democratic government can come into being. Wherever in a democracy such deep clefts between groups arise, that democracy is already doomed. Under these conditions there are only two alternatives—the rule of an external conqueror or of a strong-arm man from within, a dictator of some sort. Democracy needs consensus. Consensus means an integrated society within which the internal conflicts are subordinated to the common loyalty, the will for unity. Venezuela exhibited the divisiveness of racial groups that characterized, in different degrees, all the countries of Latin America, and these groups constituted at the same time a social stratification, an order of domination and subjection. Thus the conditions were set for the coming to power of a careerist such as Guzmán Blanco. To understand the special features of his regime, however, and to understand the peculiar character of caudillo rule we shall have to probe much more thoroughly into the whole situation.

The aborigines in Venezuela at the time of the conquest differed from those in Mexico and Peru in two important respects. First, they were less numerous, being more sparsely settled in relation to the land. Second, they were much less unified. These two facts led to the eventual situation in which the Indians constituted such a small part of the nation's population that it was not a major problem. In other words, Venezuela is not today an Indian country such as Guatemala and Ecuador. But in the meantime, in the early colonial regime, the conquest of the Indians was a major concern. Precisely because the aborigines were not unified politically into an empire or a league, it was difficult to subjugate them. The Spaniards could not simply capture the governing officials and thus seize control of a unified system. Instead, they had to disperse their forces in order to wage separate wars with innumerable tribes speaking their own dialects and obedient only to their own caciques.[1] These local caciques

[1] Vallenilla Lanz, *Disgregación e integración*, pp. 118–21. Cacique: A superior in an Indian province or town; a person who in a town or district exercises excessive influence in political or administrative matters. Real Academia Española, *Diccionario de la lengua española*, p. 212.

seldom conducted open warfare, but they did use effective guerrilla tactics. The country accordingly had to be conquered by inches with the help of courage, patience, and privation. The early struggle with the aborigines in dispersed areas over the country was perhaps one of the primary factors in giving Venezuela a localistic tendency, later to become evident in the political scene.

The Indians of the llanos in the center of the country were the first to be either exterminated or subjugated and fused with the Spaniards racially. In other areas the struggle dragged on for many years, with subsequent fusion taking place slowly because of the *reducción*[2] system adopted by the missionaries and the settlement under the Law of the Custody of the Indians.[3] By 1810 there were still approximately one hundred and twenty thousand pure-blooded Indians in the country with much of their primitive culture intact. At that time they represented something like fifteen percent of the total population. Most of the Indian tribes supported the War of Independence, especially those in the east, where there were forty-two thousand aboriginals, most of them warlike Caribes.

The system of repartimientos and encomiendas, begun very early in the colonial regime and lasting well beyond the New Laws of 1542, was of course utilized in Venezuela.[4] It served to integrate the Indian into the Venezuelan economic system and to give him a place in the social structure, albeit a low and somewhat unrewarding one.

The disappearance of the encomienda system at the end of the seventeenth century did not free the Indians from economic obligation to their masters. They continued to pay

[2] *Reducción* meant a mission established by the church under governmental auspices. The missions exercised considerable authority over the territories to which they were assigned.

[3] Gil Fortoul, *Historia constitucional de Venezuela,* III, 63.

[4] Perera, *Historia orgánica de Venezuela,* pp. 35–41.

4

tribute to the royal exchequer through the corregidors[5] until
1811. Also, a certain proportion of Indians had long been
placed on communal lands, or *resguardos,* which in Venezuela were not broken up into private Indian properties until
the order of May 20, 1820, was put into effect in 1836.[6]

The other influence which greatly affected the Indians was
the missionaries, who began their work in Venezuela early in
the sixteenth century. Friars, coming on their own initiative
and receiving no aid, accompanied the conquerors with the
aim of evangelizing the savages. The first bishopric of Venezuela was established at Coro in 1531, and missionaries appeared there and in Guiana at an early date. The system of
missions, however, was not instituted until 1652 by Philip II.
He granted to the Capuchins of Aragon a large part of the
province of Cumaná. In 1658 the Capuchins were also established in the province of Caracas.

In Cumaná the Franciscan Observants were granted the
region of Píritu. They were also given the central Orinoco
region. After 1664 this region was entered by Franciscans,
Augustinians, Jesuits, Dominicans, and Capuchins, but most
had deserted it by the end of the seventeenth century because of the absence of means of subsistence in this isolated
region and the unhealthfulness of the climate. In 1736 the territory of Venezuela was divided among the Capuchins, the
Franciscans, and the Jesuits. There were frequent disputes
between the orders over the respective territorial limits.
These disputes contributed to the turbulence of the colonial
life.[7]

The missions, whose original purpose was to convert the
Indians, not only applied themselves to this task and gave

[5] Corregidor: A magistrate or councilman who by royal appointment
exercised in his territory municipal, administrative, and judicial functions.
Real Academia Española, *Diccionario de la lengua española,* p. 357.
[6] Perera, *Historia orgánica de Venezuela,* pp. 41–42.
[7] Watters, *A History of the Church in Venezuela,* p. 7.

them some measure of civilization but also served as a political and military institution, defending the outposts from the encroachment of foreign powers and extending the territory into new lands. The state granted the missions military and financial aid. As a frontier institution, the mission moved continuously into new territory, turning its "reduced" and instructed Indians over to the secular clergy and the civil officers.

The task of reducing the Indians to the mission regime was never completed. Nature defeated the Franciscans on the upper Orinoco and the Río Negro. Others who had been reduced reverted to savagery and gave continuous trouble to the governments of Caracas and of Bogotá. Both the nomadic character of the Indian and the geography of the country defeated the objects of the missions. Lack of adequate resources and workers also retarded their work. On the whole, the missions did not receive the support of the Spanish government as did other missionaries. Venezuela suffered more from the dearth of missionaries than other parts of South America. New Granada, with two-and-a-half times the population, had more than six times as many members of the regular clergy as Venezuela. Missions frequently had to be abandoned as a result of the sudden flight of the Indians or the lack of sufficient workers.

On the north coast the missions faced the attacks of the English and French. In the province of Guayana the missions met the Dutch, the Portuguese, the French, and the English incursions. The missions also fought the encroachments of the Dutch West India Company. Even the severest critics of the mission system recognize its service to Spain and to Venezuela as an institution of territorial expansion and defense of frontiers.

Practically all the towns founded in Venezuela during the colonial period owed their origins to the missionary. The real work of colonization was done by him, since the military and civilian agencies had failed to occupy the country after a century of effort. The Indians within the mission were allowed to choose certain local officials from their number, but the individuals selected functioned under the absolute rule of the missionary, thus being trained for civil life.

Each mission had a common farm worked by the Indians and plots that the natives worked for themselves. The Indians, overworked and underpaid, exploited in the sale of rosaries and images, and kept in reductions against their natural tendency toward nomadic life, developed a hatred toward monks and Spaniards in general.

The failure to achieve the permanent social salvation of the Indian may be attributed in part to the relaxation of discipline in the orders in the 18th century and local dissensions and rebellions against superiors and, in some instances, to the exploitation of the Indian by the missionary. Whatever the cause, the result was significant for the future of the church under the Republic. With the abolition of the missions in the revolutionary epoch, the control of the church over the Indian was lost. He became either hostile because of hatred toward the missionary, or indifferent through the failure of the church to make a permanent impression on his mind. The civilizing effect of the mission disappeared with them.[8]

Beginning in 1510, by special dispensation of the crown, Negroes were imported into Venezuela in sizable numbers. It was ironical that Las Casas, the man who did most among the Christian missionaries to improve the lot of the Indian, was the one responsible for the introduction of Negro slaves into Venezuela. He suggested in 1510 that permission be given for twelve Negro slaves to be brought to Venezuela. As soon as the door was thus opened, instead of twelve, over three hundred were brought. Subsequent importations in-

[8] *Ibid.*, p. 30.

creased the number of Negroes so that by about 1812 there were, according to one authority, some sixty thousand Negro slaves in Venezuela, forty thousand of whom lived in the province of Caracas. This would mean about seven percent of the total population.[9] There were a number of laws promulgated by the Spanish crown to protect slaves against exploitation, but these laws were a medley of coddling measures which would have provided the Negro slaves with greater comfort than most poor whites enjoyed and, on the other hand, prescriptions for severe corporal punishment, with details as to how and when it was to be imposed. Thus, the orders of the crown directed that the owners of slaves build special separate houses for both sexes with high beds and silk covers, and that no more than two should be placed in any one room; but at the same time these rules made provision for punishment by prison or by whipping, so long as the whipping was not done around the head and so long as no grave contusion or flow of blood resulted from the whipping. Of course, as in the case of the Indians, these regulations were interpreted by the owners of the slaves to their own satisfaction. No attention was paid to the special luxury provisions of the protective laws for the slaves, nor on the other hand, were the restrictions on punishment taken very seriously. The laws were, in fact, administered for the benefit of the masters. Humboldt observes:

The civil authority is impotent wherever it refers to domestic slavery and nothing is more illusory than to expect special effect from laws which prescribe the form of treatment and the number of blows that can be given at any time.[10]

[9] Gil Fortoul, *Historia constitucional de Venezuela*, I, 76. Tannenbaum, *Slave and Citizen*, p. 13, says that, "Toward the end of the colonial period, Venezuela, in a population of approximately 1,000,000 had 72,000 Negro slaves and 400,000 Mulattoes, or something over 47 percent of African origin."
[10] *Voyage aux régions équinoxiales du nouveau continent*, IV, 183.

Under these conditions color became a perennial mark of inferiority. Negroes, whether slaves or free, were compelled to marry only among themselves. Negro women or mulattoes were forbidden to dress in silk or to wear gold or pearls. They were not allowed to have Indians in their service. They were not allowed to carry arms and they were not permitted to walk the streets at night. These laws, of course, could not prevent the crossing of blood and it was possible to distinguish seven separate castes in the Oriental Indies.

1. The Spaniards born in Europe.
2. The Spaniards born in America, who were known as creoles.
3. The mestizos, descendants of whites and Indians.
4. The mulattoes, descendants of whites and Negroes.
5. The zambos, descendants of Indians and Negroes.
6. The Indians.
7. The Negroes.

In Venezuela all persons who were not of pure white race were called pardos, a caste which at the end of the colonial time comprised half of the total population.[11] There was continuous racial conflict among the various groups. The whites, who controlled the land in large holdings, owned tribute from the Indians through the repartimientos and encomiendas, and owned the Negroes who were working in their mines, looked with great fear upon the multiplication of the mestizo class and opposed mestizo social demands until the eve of the revolution. An act of the ayuntamiento of Caracas, dated April 14, 1796, reveals how bitter the fight was between the whites and the mixed races. On that day the Royal Decree, issued on February 10, 1795, was considered by the body in Caracas. The decree provided for special arrangements whereby the pardos could obtain special dispen-

---

[11] Baralt, *Resumen de la historia de Venezuela*, p. 361.

sation from their class on payment of certain fees which entitled them to equality with the whites and to certain titles. The petition said:

Should the pardos be freed of their status they would be able to compete for offices in the republic which belong to white persons, and they would succeed in occupying such government posts without any impediment, mixing and being equal with the whites and people of greatest distinction in the republic; in this case no one will be willing to serve in public offices, such as the regidores, and the hacienda and the treasury will suffer greatly.

The petition also points out:

That dissensions and difficulties will arise among the respective classes of the republic should the dispensation be given to the pardos. Since they compose the larger part of the population and also have a great natural increase, and since they are ambitious for honors and anxious to become equal with the whites in spite of the inferior class in which Providence has placed them, they will create difficulties in the country.

The act continues:

The transition of the pardos to the same status as the whites would be very shocking for the native born of America, because they have known since birth or from many years of experience the great distance separating white from pardo, the advantage and the superiority of the white ones, and the low qualities and subordination of the pardos.

The petition further strikes out against:

The freeing of the pardos and against making possible for them learning which they have lacked until now and which they should lack in the future. The effect would be to populate the classes of students with mulattoes. They will even attempt to enter in the seminary. They will occupy offices of councillors, they will serve in public offices and in the royal treasury, and the sad days will come when Spain, because of the force of the pardos, will see itself served by mulattoes, zambos, and Negroes whose suspected fidelity will cause violent commotions.

Other provisions distinguished between the pardos who lived in the city and who would attempt to change their lot and their life to be equal with the whites, and the few who still lived in the country and were more retiring and obedient. It further pointed out that the pardos who live in the city are artisans. They are carpenters, silversmiths, tailors, masons, shoemakers, butchers, and other mechanics who decide for themselves when to work and how to work and who place a high price on their labor and are also cheating the public at all times. Others are sergeants and corporals in the militia who, instead of cultivating the land, display their official status and enjoy their position in the army. Finally, even those who do come to work in the camp in the country are fools and liars who obtain loans from the owners of the hacienda and then find an excuse to leave their work. In conclusion, the petition suggests the following remedies:

1. That the pardos be obliged to work the land.
2. That there should be a definite regulation of their works and there should be a price placed on their labor; that the militia of whites and pardos be separated so that they could serve properly should any public disturbances occur; and that the pardos should be discouraged from any thoughts of advancement.[12]

This petition has been quoted rather extensively because it indicates the spirit of the conflict among the races which existed some fifteen years before independence. It was this distinction and this continuous conflict which continued to plague Venezuela after independence was achieved.

It is interesting to note that the conflict existed not only

[12] Gil Fortoul, *Historia constitucional de Venezuela*, I, 79–82.

between the creoles and the pardos but also between two white groups, the creoles and the peninsular people who were sent from Spain for definite periods to Venezuela. The creoles, who owned most of the land and who made their wealth an instrument of dominance, were afraid that the people coming from Spain would undermine their influence. While it is true that the Spanish crown was interested in the financial advantages derived from granting titles, it nevertheless had to extend certain protection to the pardos and mestizos; this was one of the main reasons for contention between the creoles and the peninsulars. In reply to the petition of Caracas, quoted above, the captain-general of Venezuela, disregarding the petition, published on March 9, 1802, a tariff which enabled the pardos to change their status by payment of certain amounts of money. Upon payment of six thousand reales, sons of unknown fathers could obtain the office of *escribano,* corresponding to secretary. To become a hidalgo, one had to pay one hundred and seven thousand reales. For the price of fifteen hundred reales, one could obtain the distinctive title of don, and upon payment of seven hundred reales, a pardo could change his status and become the equal of the whites.[13]

A number of pardos who worked as artisans and as merchants had the means to buy their new status and availed themselves of the privilege to a large extent. This both infuriated and intimidated the creoles, who became concerned over the maintenance of their superiority in the country. Since it was the crown who allowed this change of status by payment of money and since the Spanish representatives who came to Venezuela supported the pardos in their change of status and extended protection to all the races, the conflict between the creoles and the peninsulars became intensified toward the close of the colonial times.

[13] *Ibid.,* I, 82.

The creoles had one more serious preoccupation. It consisted of being able to prove their own racial purity and their own claims to nobility. The majority of the hidalgos were non-Spanish. They acquired their rank and their title during the wars and in adventures of conquest. Many of them became nobles because they took advantage of the financial straits in which the Spanish court lived those years. It was possible to buy a title and a rank in the army. Inasmuch as the creoles were the only ones who had large landholdings and extensive wealth, they were in the market for the titles but, nevertheless, were always envious of the Spanish peninsulars who had titles that had come down to them from their aristocratic forefathers. Not very certain of the purity of their own blood, the creoles of the seventeenth and eighteenth centuries were trying hard to prove it by constructing meticulous records. They had to prove that they were:

Spaniards, old Christians, free from any mixture of the bad races of the Moors, Jews, and mulattoes; that they were not heretics and were not newly converted to the Holy Church; that they had not been jailed by the sacred office of the Inquisition or by any other tribunal; that no punishment had been imposed upon them which could deprive them of their honor; that they had not held vile or mechanical offices in the republic; and that they had always been esteemed and accepted as gentlemen hidalgos and that, as such, they had obtained their first post in the service of the republic in their places of residence.[14]

Considering the great mixture of blood that was taking place in Venezuela, the miscegenation of the creoles with Indian mestizos and Negro women and the official sexual unions between the hidalgos and Indians which was per-

[14] Información de limpieza de sangre de Francisco Rodríguez, Marqués del Toro, 1744, Archivos de Caracas, cited by Gil Fortoul, *Historia constitucional de Venezuela,* I, 86.

mitted by the law, one must assume that a large number of creoles who pretended that they had pure Spanish blood were actually mestizos or pardos. The crown, however, was willing to accept their claims and issued titles to them, especially since many of the peninsulars who had Arabic blood in their veins looked much browner and darker than the creoles or even than some mestizos. Plainly the fundamental basis for the dominant creole class as the oligarchy of the colony was military glory in the conquest and riches acquired through the division of land and the exploitation of the Indians and slaves. It should also be taken into account, however, that even the creoles had access only to certain municipal offices. They could not hold high public, judicial, military, or ecclesiastical offices and as their strength and their ambition grew, their envy and conflict with the Spanish increased. Their personal desire for advancement was one of the principal motives of the revolution.

At the end of the colonial regime there were approximately in Venezuela twelve thousand Spaniards, two hundred thousand creoles, and four hundred and six thousand mixed people.[15] They were castes which hated each other, both because of the diversity of their origin and because of the lack of equality of their conditions. Other groups included the one hundred and twenty thousand Indians who, although protected by law, were in fact reduced to slavery by the encomiendas, the missionaries, and the proprietors of lands. The Negroes, also theoretically protected by social legislation, suffered abject slavery in the mines and on the estates. Poor pardos were excluded from the municipal government and were victims of the antagonism of the white creoles, who were interested only in lazily enjoying the riches of their grandfathers and the titles bought from the crown. Finally,

[15] Baralt, *Resumen de la historia de Venezuela*, p. 361.

the peninsulars, mostly public employees who, although not favorably disposed toward the mixed races, nevertheless found a chance for their own advancement in the conflicts between the domestic castes. They were, therefore, not really interested in reconciling the class differences.

CHAPTER II

THE INSTITUTIONAL STRUCTURE
OF COLONIAL VENEZUELA

A REVIEW OF THE CONTROLLING INSTITUTIONS of Spanish Venezuela shows that they were all based on the same assump-
tions, an attitude toward the land as a basis of exploitation,
an acceptance of the caste system, rigidity, and a lack of any
principle of unity. It is important to realize the significance
of these conditions when we seek to understand how a man
like Guzmán Blanco came to power and how he ruled when
power was, rather precariously, in his hands.

Colonial Venezuela suffered from divisiveness in all its
structure and not least in the political framework. Unlike
other Spanish dependencies, which had an effective central
government either under a viceroy or a captain general, the
Venezuelan territory consisted first of six, then later of seven,
provinces ruled by individual governors who, in effect, recognized no central authority other than the distant crown, even
during the short-lived period (1777–1810) when the governor
of Caracas was designated, without much actual power, also
as captain general of the entire territory. Furthermore, the
six or seven provinces were actually, with the exception of
the province of Guayana, extensions of six cities—the provinces having taken in five cases the names of the cities and
the government of the cities being the ultimate dominating
factor for each province insofar as Venezuela was concerned.
The entire political history of Venezuela, including its subsequent history when independent, was greatly influenced
by this fact. The extreme localism which the arrangement

engendered is to be seen from the fact that neither the governors of the individual provinces nor the governor of Caracas, when he was designated as captain general, could exercise any real authority over their own individual provinces or over the entire territory of Venezuela.

The provinces in Venezuela had, to some extent, the classical structure imposed throughout colonial Spain. The crown was the supreme authority. The highest judicial and ecclesiastical authority was vested in the audiencias, first in that of Santo Domingo, later also in that of Santa Fé and, during the last thirty years of colonial regime, in Caracas. There were governors appointed by the crown, and, beginning in 1777, a captain general of the entire territory for a period of seven years. There were intendants appointed for economic and fiscal matters in the second half of the eighteenth century.[1] But outside of the distant crown, these superior bodies had little actual authority over the provinces of Venezuela. The audiencias in Santo Domingo and Santa Fé were too far away. Poor communications and expensive and tedious transportation discouraged too frequent contact with the audiencias. The intendants and the captain general, when they came into being in the latter part of the eighteenth century, lasted too short a time to exert any real influence, either during the last years of the colonial regime or during independence.

The two acknowledged elements of government in the history of colonial Venezuela were the office of the governor of the province and the cabildo or ayuntamiento.[2] Politically Venezuela was divided into the provinces of Caracas, Mérida, Maracaibo, Cumaná, Marguerita, and Guayana, to which in 1794 was added the province of Barcelona. At the head of

[1] Baralt, *Resumen de la historia de Venezuela.*
[2] A body composed of a mayor and several councilmen for the administration of a municipality. Real Academia Española, *Diccionario de la lengua española,* p. 146.

each provincial government was a governor. The governors and the captain general were dependent upon the Council of the Indies, created in 1542 by the authority of the king, which had supreme jurisdiction in the Western Indies.

The prerogatives of the governors and, later, of the captain general of the province of Caracas, were very limited. As the conquest of Venezuela was completed, the military function of the governor, who was also commander in chief of the small Spanish garrison, practically came to an end. The term of the governor was for five years and that of the captain general, seven years. During their term of office their personal and political life was circumscribed first by royal regulations, second by the autonomous ambitions of the cabildo, and third by the fact that after they completed their term they were subject to a judicial investigation and were held responsible for any mismanagement of their office. Their private life was regulated as follows:

No governor could have more than four slaves throughout the entire province; he could not enter into business; neither he nor his sons could marry; he could not attend weddings or funerals nor could he act as godfather at christenings.[3]

The governor was in charge of political and military administration, and where there were no cabildos he could appoint justices in townships. He was also entrusted with the political relations between his province and the colonial institutions of foreign powers. He could attend sessions of the cabildos but without the right to take part in deliberations or to vote. Although he was the representative of the royal interests in the province, with the establishment of the offices of intendants he lost the supervision of the affairs of the royal treasury. The intendants were in exclusive charge of fiscal administrations and of receiving and dis-

[3] Vallenilla Lanz, *Disgregación e integración*, p. 14.

tributing the contributions imposed by the crown, and they supervised all financial and administrative matters connected with finances in complete independence of the governor or of the captain general. Actually, with the reduction of the military forces to small garrisons or militia, the governors were limited to supervision of the enforcement of the royal decrees. They did not enjoy the vast political and judicial prerogatives of the audiencias and cabildos, they had no control over fiscal or economic matters, and they were even hampered in the naming of the bureaucracy of the provinces. The final accounting of their administration had to be made before a delegate appointed by the Council of the Indies. For sixty consecutive days this delegate accepted complaints against the governor from official bodies and individual citizens. After receiving the complaints, this delegate took another sixty days to investigate them and send his disposition to the Council of the Indies, which rendered the final verdict. In some cases the final judgment was rendered by the audiencia. In 1590 the ayuntamiento of Caracas petitioned the king to permit the audiencia in Santo Domingo to render the final verdict on the conduct of the governors since, in the words of their petition, "It would be too far for the claimants to go to Spain to appear before the Council of the Indies and, therefore, the final judgment of the governors should be issued by the audiencia."

The few prerogatives of the governors of the provinces, and even of the captain general, and the control imposed by the audiencias and residencias constituted the classical example of checks and balances characteristic of the Spanish colonial rule. In addition to those political limitations which curbed any centralist tendencies of the governors, there were the natural geographic and topographical barriers which militated against the concentration of power in the hands of any governor or captain general. It is, therefore, apparent that the administration of the governors of the several provinces and of the captain general did not lend to any unification of the provinces of the territory of Venezuela and was not instrumental in either encouraging or in imposing a system of centralized government on colonial Venezuela.

Of greater and far more lasting importance was the second element of the colonial political structure—that of the cabildo or ayuntamiento. Transposed from Spain to colonial Venezuela, this cabildo, as in Spain, was the expression of both local autonomy and of opposition to centralist rule. The institution of the cabildo was brought to Venezuela with the beginning of the Spanish conquest. Juan de Solórzano de Pereira in his *Política indiana* states:

It was ordered that in cities and places which the Spaniards were founding and populating, there should be introduced at the same time the competent, prudent, political government which will be required and that there should be established the institutions of cabildos, regidores, and the other necessary officials for such republics, who should each year elect among their own neighbors their judges—ordinary mayors—who, during the term of their office and within their territory, should preside over civil and criminal jurisdiction with the same right as if they would have been named by the king himself.[4]

From the very beginning the cabildos were given wide latitude. Since the audiencias of both Santo Domingo and Bogotá were very far away, the cabildos assumed most of the administrative prerogatives of the audiencias. In addition to administration, the alcaldes were in charge of the judicial power. The position of the alcaldes became strengthened when, by royal decree in 1560, they were named by the crown to serve as interim governors of the provinces whenever the governor died or was absent from his post. This served further to identify the province with the city, since

[4] I, 252.

the alcaldes were elected by the members of the cabildo.

When the townships and cities were founded, the governors named the cabildos which consisted of either eight or four councilmen known as the regidores. When the territories were conquered and the cities firmly established, the office of regidor became hereditary and could be bought by and sold to members of the creole class. The appointment not being dependent any more on the good will of the founding military chiefs, who also became governors, the regidores soon turned upon them.

The cabildos attempted to curb the already greatly limited power of the governor and many times found support from the crown. The conflict between the governors and the cabildos became more pronounced when certain families, entrenched as regidores carried on the policy of exclusivism known in Venezuela as *mantuanismo*. This policy consisted of keeping the offices of regidores within certain families and also resulted in blocking the drive of the colored races and of the half-castes for emancipation and participation in the cabildos. In a previous section we have discussed the petition sent by the ayuntamiento of Caracas against the pardos. Since for political and economic interests of the crown it was incumbent upon the governors to protect the rights of the mixed races, the struggle between the cabildos and the governors became ever more intense toward the end of the colonial period.

The *mantuanismo,* or the policy of keeping the offices of the regidores and, therefore, the control of the city government in the hands of a few families, resulted in the creation of an oligarchy whose hold on the office and whose arbitrary conduct with regard to the emancipation of the population was much stronger than the hold of the Spanish colonial rule. As the provinces of Venezuela were approaching independence, the position of the cabildos was practically supreme. The head of the Spanish expeditionary forces, Lieutenant General Don Pablo Morillo, reported to the government of Spain as follows in 1816:

It is necessary, Your Excellency, that you should be aware of the fact that the cabildos of the capitals of the provinces have the power to order other townships of the provinces as if they were the captain-general of their district, despite the fact that there are towns more centrally located than the one where there is a cabildo; the result is that the cabildo is not the municipal authority for one city but the government for the entire province.[5]

Another example in confirmation of Morillo's statement is the case of the city of Barcelona. In 1793 it wanted to be elevated to the category of a province and the ayuntamiento of Barcelona sent a petition to the king, who granted this request. When the governor of the province of Cumaná, to which Barcelona belonged, filed a brief with the king opposing the request, he was suspended and ordered to appear before the audiencia of Caracas.[6]

Thus, the heritage of the political structure of the provinces of Venezuela on the eve of independence contained two conflicting principles. On the one hand, there was the emasculated attempt at central government represented by the much abused, much controlled, and much investigated Spanish governors. On the other hand, there was a strongly entrenched localist municipal oligarchy, jealous of its power and opposed to any encroachment on the part of a central authority. The latter were the exponents of restrictive class rule, bent upon retaining this coveted municipal autonomy within a limited number of families who were hostile to the desire for freedom and emancipation on the part of the racially mixed and economically inferior classes.

In colonial Spanish America the Church was a powerful

[5] Pons, *Voyage . . . dans l'Amerique méridionale*, III, 188.
[6] Rodríguez Villa, *El Teniente General don Pablo Morillo*, III, 166.

part of the social and political order for several reasons. First, it was so closely identified with the Spanish crown through the *real patronato de las Indias* that its interests were one with the strengthening of Spanish rule. Its officials, for example, sometimes held ecclesiastical and governmental positions at the same time.[7] Second, in virtue of its close connection with the crown, the Church held a monopoly in religious affairs, and both it and the crown were bent upon maintaining and strengthening this monopoly through various kinds of controls over the population. Third, the Church was a large-scale economic institution in that it held large amounts of land and received sizable revenues both from governmental and private sources. Fourth, as a means of carrying on its religious monopoly, its economic position, and its alliance with the crown, the Church performed many functions that today are thought of as lying within the province of government, such as education, care of the aborigines, censorship of books and ideas, and administration of revenues.

Naturally, the Venezuelan situation reflected these characteristics of the Church in the colonies. There the Church was a major institution and the clergy a powerful class. Because it had within its own organization a gradation of ranks and a variety of societies, it by no means presented a wholly united front or always played a unitary role in political affairs or in the class structure. Its activities were complex but, nevertheless, important in the social order.

The work of the regular clergy in missionary endeavor, the control of the aboriginals, and the defense of the frontier has already been mentioned. It should be pointed out that the Church also served as the source and center of educa-

[7] Simpson, *Many Mexicos,* Chap. XV. The background and complicated character of the *patronato* are described by Mecham, *Church and State in Latin America.* Chap. I.

tion in colonial Venezuela. Primary schools were organized in Caracas soon after the founding of the city in 1567, but by 1591 only one such school remained. A seminary and a school of grammar were established in 1592. Although these were secular, the clergy were the primary agents in the promotion of education. Three convent schools were established in the seventeenth century, with chairs of theology, ethics, and philosophy. The seminary of Santa Rosa was opened in 1692 and was entirely under the direction of the episcopate. Primary schools were under the direction of priests. The first school for girls was established in Caracas by Father Malpica. The Royal and Pontifical University of Caracas, founded in 1721, was controlled by ecclesiastics. Venezuela, however, did not have educational institutions equal to those of Mexico and Peru, since her population and her resources did not justify and could not support wider educational facilities. The Church controlled education not only in colonial times but also well into the republic. It was one of the distinctions of Guzmán Blanco that, in 1870, he for the first time introduced compulsory, free elementary education. Under his regime a number of secular academies and institutions were established.

In the colonial and early republican periods the schools controlled by the Church were attended mainly by children of the peninsular and creole classes. Both the Indians and the slaves remained uneducated except as they were instructed in the missions. The religious control of education thus helped to foster loyalty to Church and crown among all classes.

Economically, the power of the Church and its connection with the government can be seen from the fact that, at the end of the colonial regime, the annual income from tithes was 414,215 pesos. This sum was divided as follows: One-quarter to the archbishop or bishop, as the case might be;

one-quarter to the cabildo; one-sixth for the maintenance of churches; one-ninth to the king; and two-ninths for the salary of the clergy or, if any was left over, to the cabildo.[8]

In view of the economic and social position of the Church, it is natural that sons of the families of highest social rank sought places in the ecclesiastical organization. While the bishops were usually Spanish, many of the higher clergy were creoles. The first archbishop, Ibarra, was a native Venezuelan.

The episcopate was distinguished on the whole by the secular aspiration of its incumbents, their desire to secure the dominance of society and even the civil control of the country in competition with the political authorities. Distinction in civil office was, to be sure, common in the Spanish colonial churchmen. Monarchs entrusted to them many political functions; indeed, they often filled the highest places in the government as viceroys, judges of the audiencias, and governors of provinces. Ecclesiastics, it is true, did not hold civil office in Venezuela as frequently as the clergy did in other divisions of the empire, but they attained, through their ecclesiastical position alone, a political power as well as a social influence comparable to that exercised in any other jurisdiction. Indeed, they are equalled in their individuality, their unique character and their remarkable statesmanship, only by the interesting group of churchmen found in colonial Chile.[9]

Within the Church itself, however, there prevailed decentralization and factionalism that was so characteristic of Venezuelan society. The Church was rampant with bitter conflicts between the regular and secular clergy and between the separate orders and units of secular organizations. These dissensions lessened the political and social effectiveness of the Church as a whole. Spain's neglect of Venezuela (since it was not a producer of gold like other South American

[8] Gil Fortoul, *Historia constitucional de Venezuela*, I, 97.
[9] Watters, *A History of the Church in Venezuela*, p. 40.

countries) and its general poverty had an adverse effect on the Church. Its personnel was always inadequate and its wealth never equalled that of other South American countries or of Mexico.

In the local dissensions in the orders and rebellions against the authority of the provincials, one finds in the Church illustrations of the disunity of Venezuelan society. This lack of unity in the clergy was particularly notable in the War of Independence.

The ecclesiastical organization in Venezuela, as well as the political, furnished a most intriguing instance of that characteristic decentralization in Spanish colonial administration. In no other division of the Empire, it is thought, could such a lack of integration be found. The completion of unification only at the very close of the colonial period left its heritage of division and factionalism to the national Church as well as to the state.[10]

The economic institutions of colonial Venezuela were the expression of the mercantilist interests of the metropolitan country and the feudal interests of the colonial aristocracy. The peninsulars were the chief representatives of the former interests, and the owners of the great estates of the latter. The economic welfare of the colony itself was entirely subordinated to these interests. No serious attempt was made to develop its economy as a whole. The system of social stratification, in which caste lines tended to coincide with racial and color lines, introduced an additional factor calculated to encourage a kind of economic immobility in which the ambitions of the more powerful were directed more toward spoliation and domination than to healthy enterprise.

The crown, the peninsulars, and the creoles were all, in their several ways, responsible for this condition. In their official capacity the peninsulars received directly the taxes

[10] *Ibid.*, pp. 31–32.

on the mines and on the customs houses, the tributes from the Indians, and even the ecclesiastical levy. They supervised the exploitation of the mines and, during the time when commerce with Spain was the direct monopoly of the crown, these peninsulars also received the shipments arriving from Europe and disposed of them in the local markets.

Although the ownership of the mines was in the hands of the conquerors and their descendants (now the creoles), these had to pay to the crown, first one-half of the income, later one-third, and finally one-fifth.[11] The royal representatives handled the commerce on behalf of the crown during its monopoly, but they had to depend for distribution and sale of merchandise on the mestizos and pardos because the creoles considered it beneath their dignity to have stores. Also, under the orders of the crown, Moors, Jews, new converts, and foreigners were excluded from trading. Since trading then fell to the lot of the mestizos and pardos, this gave them their first economic hold, which in later years came to plague the creoles and the landed aristocracy.

After the Venezuelan territory was subjugated, the conquerors and their descendants who had acquired mines wherever possible and who had become large landowners and holders of repartimientos and encomiendas, lived from the work of the Indians on the land and the Negro slaves in the mines. There was no interest and no attempt to develop industries. Furthermore, the Spanish system did not encourage independent industrial developments in the colonies but restricted colonial manufacturers in every way, particularly with regard to items that might compete with the output of Spanish cities and merchants who were the beneficiaries of the crown's exclusive monopoly for trading in the colonies.[12]

[11] Gil Fortoul, *Historia constitucional de Venezuela*, Vol. I.
[12] Baralt, *Resumen de la historia de Venezuela*, p. 391.

Shipping was restricted to Spanish vessels plying between Santo Domingo and the Venezuelan ports.[13] The choice of cargo taken from Venezuela depended on the interests of the crown and not on the agricultural produce of Venezuela. As far back as 1590 Simón de Bolívar, the procurator-general of the province of Caracas, who incidentally was the first member of the Bolívar family to establish himself there, sent a memorandum to the Council of the Indies asking for a number of improvements in the economic regulations which governed Venezuela. Among these figured the request that permission be granted for two boats of Sevilla or Cádiz registry to come directly from Spain with the merchandise required for the supply of the province because, he claimed, this province was outside of the general navigation of the fleets of the crown.[14]

This petition was rejected, and for another century Venezeula had to depend on trans-shipment through Santo Domingo for its commerce with Spain. Even in the beginning of the eighteenth century, for the fifteen years between 1706 and 1721, not a single boat came directly from Spain to the ports of La Guaira, Puerto Cabello, or Maracaibo.[15] This attitude on the part of the crown encouraged illegal trade, contraband and smuggling being carried on primarily by the Dutch from Curaçao, who had succeeded in creating their own monopoly of the commerce with the ports of Venezuela. To combat this contraband, Philip V prohibited on November 1, 1717, and again on June 9, 1718, the importation to Spain of fruits grown in Venezuela which were transported in foreign boats. To induce Spanish shipping to go to Venezuela directly to import cocoa, he removed the duty on the tonnage on such boats. Also, to win the Venezuelans away

[13] *Ibid.*, p. 401.
[14] Gil Fortoul, *Historia constitucional de Venezuela*, I, 103.
[15] Baralt, *Resumen de la historia de Venezuela*, p. 364.

from the contraband trading with the Dutch, he reduced the import duties on cocoa by fifty-six percent. These measures, however, were not effective and brought little change in the situation.

The first major change in the trade situation, a change which, although opposed at the beginning, proved to be an advantage in the economic development of Venezuela, was an agreement made on September 25, 1728, with the Guipuzcoana Company. The first article of the agreement gave the company the monopoly on commerce with the province of Caracas and Guipúzcoa in Spain. The contract also authorized the captains of the company's boats to hunt down and, if possible, to suppress all illegal traffic on the coasts of the province. Secondly, the boats of the company were allowed to load merchandise for Venezuela in the ports of Guipúzcoa without paying any duties on the tonnage. Instead, before leaving Spain for America, the boats had to pay five percent exit duty and two per cent entrance duty, which, under previous arrangements, they would have had to pay at Cádiz. Upon returning, the boats were required to stop at Cádiz but could continue on later to Guipúzcoa with a part of their cargo. Provision was made that merchandise, gold, and silver which the boats of the company would confiscate from the illegal traffickers were to be sold in the Indies without any sales tax. The proceeds of such sales were to be divided, with two-thirds going to the company and those who financed it and one-third to the officers and the crews of their boats. The company was permitted to supply the provinces of Cumaná, Trinidad, and Marguerita whenever there were no other direct boats from Spain in those places.[16]

The company began operations on July 15, 1730, when two boats and two frigates left for Venezuela. In that year the

[16] *Ibid.*, pp. 413–14.

company began to establish a number of trading centers, first in Caracas, then at La Guaira, Puerto Cabello, Coro, and Maracaibo. It appears also that the directors of the company had a more practical sense than most other Spaniards, because in 1737 they sent a special commission to Caracas to investigate whether their local director, Nicolás de Francia, had established the proper accounting in the trading centers and also to ascertain the status of the accounts and the quality of the existing merchandise. The commission was especially charged with learning the requirements of the natives as far as provisions and clothing were concerned so that they could be fulfilled through the boats of the company. And finally, the commission was charged to investigate whether the behavior of the directors of all the trading centers was proper with regard to the dependents and employees of the trading centers and whether the directors lived in a Christian way.

The control of the company was held by King Philip V, who owned five hundred shares valued at one hundred thousand pesos. One hundred shares were held by the province of Guipúzcoa. In later years leading families from Caracas, such as the families of Toro, Bolívar, Ibarra, Tovar, and others, held shares in the company. The profits were very satisfactory, reaching in a relatively short time one hundred and sixty percent of the invested capital.[17]

The activities of the company were of a decided benefit to the commerce of Spain and to Venezuela. The boats of the company brought not only merchandise, they brought books, ideas, manifestations of an enterprising spirit, and men imbued with the ideas of improvements which were to culminate in the French Revolution. The influence of the men of Guipúzcoa, who were close neighbors of France and who

[17] Gil Fortoul, *Historia constitucional de Venezuela*, I, 109.

frequently demonstrated practical energies and a spirit of independence, helped to modernize the antiquated life and viewpoint of the descendants of the conquerors.

The benefits brought by this company were not limited to the growers of cocoa. About 1740 there was little coffee produced. With the new facilities for export, cultivation increased and grew to the proportions of 100,000 quintales (measure of weight of 100 kilograms) in 1808. Tobacco, the growth of which began in the sixteenth century, began to prosper and cotton also owed its development to the company, which, in 1767, brought from Martinique a French expert to develop its cultivation.

This natural economic progress initiated by the company was bound to come in conflict with the interests and prerogatives of the oligarchic class, which consisted of large landowners, descendants of the conquerors, and beneficiaries of the encomiendas. They had been accustomed for decades to a routine system of cultivation and trade which was bound to lose out against the vigorous, planned, and efficient monopoly of the company. These large landowners felt that they would lose the benefits which they had enjoyed undisturbed for many centuries. Concerned only with their own position, because their economic status determined also their political standing, they had little consideration for the general material and cultural progress of the country.

Since they considered themselves threatened by the company, they provoked in 1749 and 1751 attacks against the company and its representatives, which led to open revolt against the governor of Caracas and the representatives of the Crown. For a while the position of the company's representatives was precarious, but the crown soon took energetic action against the instigators of these attacks and the leader of the open rebellion, Juan Francisco de León, was taken to Spain to stand trial.

That there were no real reasons for the conflict between the landowners and the company, except the desire of the former to retain their hegemony over the economy of Venezuela, is proven by the fact that later some of the members of the cabildo of Caracas, such as Toro, Bolívar, Tovar, and Ascanio, who supported de León in his fight against the company in 1749, are found among the shareholders of the very same company in 1760.[18]

Thus again, there was demonstrated the basic traits of the class stratification in Venezuela. These landowners found in their attack upon the company a means of expressing their resentment against the peninsulars who were embodied in the Spanish representatives of the company in Venezuela as well as their decided opposition to the economic emancipation of the other groups of the population. Since they themselves looked with contempt on trade and traders, these functions had to be assumed under the supervision of the company agents and by other ethnic groups such as the mestizos and pardos, who in these new occupations open to them, found the means for their economic improvement and social emancipation. To maintain their own superior status and the inferior position of the mixed races, these creole landowners would not hesitate to attack one of the most important agencies in the economic and cultural awakening of Venezuela.

The economic development of other provinces was not as intensive as that of Caracas. The province of Marguerita, with a very scant population, continued to depend on its poorly organized fishing industry. Cumaná was richer than Marguerita and enjoyed further prosperity with the initiation of the cultivation of tobacco through the influence of the Guipuzcoana Company. The province of Guiana, which, more than other provinces of Venezuela, was under the

[18] *Ibid.*, I, 110–12.

domination of the missions, attempted toward the end of the eighteenth century to rid itself of the missions, to introduce the cattle industry, and to increase its population by accepting fugitives from the Dutch and French Guianas. They were not permitted, however, to carry out these plans. Their hands were tied by the indifference of the crown and by the refusal of the missions to give up their hold on the province.

To conclude, no matter what aspect of Venezuelan society one deals with during the colonial regime, the fact of divisiveness becomes apparent. A neglected part of the Spanish Empire, sparsely populated by both aborigines and Europeans, it was characterized to a high degree by local autonomy; by class antagonisms based upon race, place of birth, and wealth; by lack of communication and education; by economic monopoly and evasion of this monopoly; and by a strife-torn clergy's control of both religious and secular functions.

Into this conflicting and unstable situation came the disturbing force of the War of Independence. Begun as a culmination of the struggle of the local oligarchy against the colonial power, this war sank to the fratricidal level of a civil war among the aroused classes, interests, and localities and ended in a temporary truce which later erupted into what is called the Federal War. It is to this later development, to a review of the basic conditions responsible for the Federal War and for the emergence of Guzmán Blanco, that we now turn.

CHAPTER III

BACKGROUND OF THE FEDERAL WAR
AND THE RISE OF GUZMÁN BLANCO

THE SAME POLITICAL AND ECONOMIC ASPECTS of Venezuelan social order apparent under the colonial regime, necessarily influenced the course of Venezuelan history during and after the struggle for independence. But, in addition to these forces, by virtue of the very fact of independence, some new issues and problems arose. One of these issues concerned the kind of government the country was to have, and here one of the major questions turned on the matter of federalism against centralism. There were reasons why this should be an issue. First, the geographical conditions tended to isolate the various cities; second, the cabildo, or local self-government, maintained throughout the colonial regime was responsible for considerable local autonomy in the isolated, but well developed communities and was an instrument and symbol of self-government; finally, the influence of the American Federal Constitution on the ideology of democratic government was a contributing cause. All of these influences sharpened the issue of federalism versus centralism in the new country. It was this issue, the focus of the present chapter, that furnished the basis of the Federal War, which, in turn, gave rise to Guzmán's career.

The strains of the sharp class differentiation in colonial Venezuela and the ever mounting conflict among the several groups were especially obvious during the last fifteen years of the colonial regime. Even though the white creoles proclaimed independence on April 19, 1810, and in the following year decreed a federal constitution which incorporated the most advanced democratic principles, such as absolute equality before the law, the substitution for titles of nobility with the common denomination of "citizen" for every Venezuelan, the elimination of caste distinction among whites, Indians, and mestizos, and the prohibition of slave trading, these very same creoles maintained their policy of separatism during the years preceding the Act of Independence and the adoption of the constitution. When these acts were officially proclaimed, therefore, the less favored races and strata had little or no confidence in the new freedoms offered to them or in the people who were guaranteeing them.

The independence movement had to rely on the creoles and on those members of mixed races who were economically dependent upon them and over whom they could exercise an immediate control. Indians who escaped from the missions, pardos who sought refuge from the discriminatory attitudes of the cabildos, and Negroes who escaped from their slavery in mines or on the land roamed the llanos engaging in pillage and murder, taking full advantage of the involvement of both the creoles and the Spanish in a sanguinary war.

However, these lowly people in the llanos did not remain destructively neutral or indifferent for very long. A crafty Spaniard, Tomás Rodríguez Boves, realizing the antagonism of these elements to the creoles and utilizing the tradition accepted among the mixed races that the Spanish government was their protector against the creoles, mobilized these forces through promises of complete freedom and of material enrichment at the expense of the hated creoles. He threw them into a war without mercy against the creole aristocracy. Before long, Boves had an army of twelve thousand to sixteen thousand daring and reckless men, who quickly turned the incipient victories of the creole fighters into defeats and who, for a number of years, carried on a war of extermination against the creoles and their partisans, literally annihilating the ranks of the creoles, especially the landed aristocracy, and completely destroying their numerical strength and political importance for the time being.[1]

The War of Independence against Spain had become a civil war among the classes in Venezuela, and although these very same llaneros were afterwards won over by General José Antonio Páez to the cause of independence and Bolívar's later campaigns succeeded in defeating the Spaniards, two important results appeared at the conclusion of the War of Independence: the creole aristocracy was eliminated from Venezuelan politics and social life; and the masses, having once gained freedom and having learned the import of their own strength, continued in ferment, either by open opposition or by guerrilla warfare, against any attempt on the part of future governments to reduce them to their pre-war stage of impotence or to deny to them the rights they had come to consider their own.

The masses, however, were not versed in political philosophy. They had, in fact, very little respect for official legislation and could not actually distinguish between the intricacies of centralist and federalist ideologies. To them force was the vehicle to power, and the individual who could, on the one hand, identify himself with their interests and, on the other hand, attract and dominate them by his personal qualities became their leader, the caudillo, the personification of power.

Communication conditions did not improve or change overnight with the achievement of independence. The large masses of the people were as isolated from the center of governmental authority as before the war. They accepted the dictum and order of their immediate caudillo and left it to

[1] Gil Fortoul, *Historia constitucional de Venezuela*, I, 316–18.

him to decide the issues for which they would or would not fight, provided he assured them the protection of their interests. Since the central government was always looked upon with distrust and ofttimes with hatred, these local caudillos, anxious to please their followers but primarily concerned with keeping themselves in power, utilized this sentiment of the masses for their own benefit and anticipated any moves of the central government which would curb their power. In their anxiety to retain their power, the caudillos became the prey of theoreticians and demagogues, visionaries and real statesmen, but the phraseology of the demagogue or the sincere statesman would not of itself have sufficed either to create internal disorder or to perpetuate it. It was the attitude of the masses and their caudillos that was responsible for the readiness of Venezuela to change theories, adopt contradicting constitutions, and engage in many wars.

The attitude and the activities of the wealthy, conservative elements which took over political control of Venezuela with the proclamation of its separation from Gran Colombia in 1830 were also responsible to a large extent for the maintenance of continuous unrest throughout the country. As we have stated earlier, the landed creole aristocracy was practically wiped out during the war. There remained in the cities, primarily in Caracas, another group of creoles, mainly of the middle class. They were merchants, professionals, and bureaucrats who, at the outbreak of the War of Independence, identified themselves with the Spanish groups because the continuation of the colonial regime would have assured them of their own standing. They did not, however, actually join the ranks of either group and had, therefore, suffered few personal losses. On the sidelines during most of the war, they took advantage in later years of the provisions of the Constitution of 1821, which pardoned people of different opinions. Also, they aligned themselves with Páez[2] during his struggle for a separate Venezuela. This group of creoles came to the fore in 1830 and immediately thereafter as the only educated and organized element in the community that could take over the government.

Their political and economic views soon became apparent with the adoption of the Constitution of 1830, which they formulated. In the attempt to retain the power of government among the property groups, they adopted a provision in the constitution, which stated:

Article 14, Section 4. To enjoy the rights of a citizen it is necessary for one . . . to be the owner of real property the annual income from which is 50 pesos, or to have a profession, an office, or a useful industry which will produce 100 pesos annually, without depending on someone else such as would be the case of a domestic servant, or to have an annual salary of 150 pesos.[3]

This provision applied to the right to vote. As far as the right of being elected to either the chamber of deputies or to the senate was concerned, the requirements were much stricter. Article 52, Section 3, of the constitution stated:

To be named a representative, one, in addition to the qualifications of a voter, must have the following . . . to be the owner of real property, the annual income from which is 400 pesos, or to have a profession, office, or useful industry which produces 500 pesos annually, or to have an annual salary of 600 pesos.[4]

To be a member of the senate, one, in addition to the qualifications of a voter, had to have these qualifications:

[2] José Antonio Páez, a general in the War of Independence, is known as the founder of Venezuela. He has already been mentioned as the man who first won over the llaneros to the cause of independence. His career will be more fully described at a later point.
[3] Constitución del estado de Venezuela, 1830, p. 5.
[4] Ibid., pp. 16–17.

Article 62, Section 4. To be the owner of real property, the annual income from which is 800 pesos, to have a profession, office, or useful industry which produces an income of 1,000 pesos annually, or to have a salary of 1,200 pesos per year.[5]

These provisions effectively curtailed the right of suffrage and limited membership in the chamber and in the senate to members of the monied classes. Having in this way assured themselves of political hegemony in the chamber and in the senate, the writers of the 1830 constitution struck out against Páez in the following provision:

Article 108. . . . The President will remain in office for four years and will not be able to be reelected immediately but only after at least one constitutional period [four years].[6]

This provision for alternation in the presidential office was introduced by the proponents of the constitution with a view toward preventing continuance in office of any one single outstanding personality. The intention was to leave for themselves the exercise of power through the economically favored actual and potential members of the national congress. In this way the oligarchy intended to protect its political domination.

Economically, the laws promulgated by this oligarchy while it was in power from 1830 to 1848 similarly favored in the extreme the affluent classes. In colonial times usury was condemned and the government regulated the rate of interest and the relation between creditor and debtor. Under the conservative oligarchy a law was passed on April 10, 1834, designated as the Law of Liberty of Contracts. Theoretically a step toward the introduction in Venezuela of the liberal views then prevalent in Great Britain, it was actually, in view of the conditions in disorganized, war-torn,

[5] *Ibid.*, p. 20.
[6] *Ibid.*, p. 27.

and economically ruined Venezuela, an attempt to grant additional economic power to the wealthy classes. This law provided as follows:

Article 1. . . . It is permissible to enter into a free contract which would provide that in order to collect the payment of any debt, the properties of the debtors will be auctioned off and sold for whatever amount will be offered for them on the day and the hour indicated for the auction.

Article 2. . . . The will of the contracting parties will be carried out with regard to any other contracts, as well as with regard to the interests which are stipulated in this contract, whatever the interest rate may be.

Article 4. . . . In the auction sales, which will take place in conformity with the disposition of Article 1 of this law, any privilege of retracting is given up and no corporation or individual will be able to claim injury or restitution in entirety.

Article 5. . . . The creditor or creditors are allowed to bid at the auction.[7]

The intent of this law and its effect are best expressed by a dissenting member of the ruling oligarchy, Fermín Toro, who published a brochure against it, which gained wide acceptance. In this brochure he says:

The liberty of contracts freed usury from all obstacles and from submission to the law. The loan business is the most lucrative of all. It is practically extended to all classes of society. The most monstrous contracts are made without blushing and the tribunals of the republic are called upon to carry them through, bringing scandal upon justice and hatred on the laws. The clamor against the law of the 10th of April was followed by far-reaching events, hatred towards the tribunals and division in the society.[8]

[7] *Recopilación de leyes*, I, 191.
[8] Gil Fortoul, *Historia constitucional de Venezuela*, II, 55.

A law aimed at the leaders of the unruly urban masses was the law of conspiracy which provided capital punishment for people convicted of conspiracy against the government.[9] In this connection, Vallenilla Lanz says in his book, *Cesarismo democrático:*

All of the laws which provided for capital punishment were carried out rigorously and very frequently, because from 1830 to 1847, the period known as the conservative one, there was not a single day of peace in Venezuela—and in the Gaceta de Venezuela of those years, one can read of the cases and of the sentences which leads us to wonder why these facts were never mentioned by the liberals in their fight against the godo party. The names in the lists were not only those of people of the llanos. There were also mulattoes and zambos. There were workers, artisans, unemployed farm hands, and a multitude of slaves who were fleeing from domination of their masters.[10]

The law of April 10, 1834, was aimed at the urban population. Other legislation of equal severity and of disruptive consequence was promulgated with regard to the rural population. One of these laws prohibited cattle stealing and provided for the severest punishment of transgressors. While in itself this law may have had a moral justification, both its intent and time of promulgation were definitely a part of the spirit of revenge against the llaneros which persisted among the creoles, whether they were members of a landed aristocracy or of a dominant middle class. Rustling of cattle was an accepted means of payment for services allowed to the llaneros first by Boves against the holdings of the Spaniards. In the plains it was not looked upon as an infamous crime, and it was condoned after the end of the war by the local caudillos who had few other means of paying their supporters. The introduction and very strict enforcement of the

[9] *Recopilación de leyes,* I, 135.
[10] Page 277.

law mentioned above and the vengeful persecution of the culprits brought bitter resentment among the people of the hinterlands and provoked the intensification of internal unrest.

A résumé of the changes in the basic Constitution of 1811 and an enumeration of the godo legislation provided for in the Constitution of 1830 is found in the manifesto of the Liberal Party of July 31, 1893. Page 2 of the manifesto states:

The first holders of power as a result of the Separatist Revolution sanctioned institutions and laws which were the reflection of their political and social ideas: a central constitution; limited suffrage; slavery; capital punishment; monopoly of education reserved for a certain class of the society; repressive and cruel legislation of the metropolis; material and economic stagnation; in one word— fear of liberty and of progress.[11]

It would seem from these facts that the civil war, rampant in the second decade of the nineteenth century and temporarily quiescent during the periods of conciliation and co-ordination of the third decade, came out again into the open during the eighteen years of the godo rule, which included the administrations of José Antonio Páez, José Vargas, and Carlos Soublette.

Until 1840, however, there was no articulate exposition of the liberal cause and no definite leadership of the Liberal Party. In that year, during the second administration of General José Páez, Antonio Leocadio Guzmán, one of Páez's strongest supporters for over a decade and a member of Páez's government in both administrations, was removed from his post because of personal differences with the Minister of Interior and Justice, Dr. José Ángel Quintero, who demanded Leocadio Guzmán's dismissal. The latter, a man of apparently great intellect, though of dubious integrity

[11] Quoted by Ruiz, *Historia patria,* p. 18.

and of opportunistic spirit, viewed his dismissal by the Secretary of Interior and Justice, who was in charge of the enforcement of the various laws discussed above, as an opportunity to become the spokesman for the opposition to the government. That same year he founded *El Venezolano*, which became the organ of the Liberal Party, and he rallied the dissatisfied elements from the various sectors of the population, integrating them into an active political movement.

The platform of the Liberal Party outlined in *El Venezolano* included rigid observance of the constitution and laws, resort to the alternating principle in filling public office, use of the electoral power with a view to converting the Liberal Party into the majority party, creation of two great national parties which, under the law, could guarantee public liberties, and the right freely to examine republican operations through public meetings and in the press.[12]

El Venezolano clarified the political situation of the country, dividing it into two strongly defined camps. Leocadio Guzmán introduced a practice heretofore unknown in Venezuela—systematized opposition. As editor of *El Venezolano*, he was the spearhead of the Liberal Party, although Laureano Vallenilla Lanz has the following to say about Antonio Leocadio's role in forming the Liberal Party:

By following a frivolous theory—that of studying social phenomena in the dim light of old theories—we see a historical axiom repeated, not only by the liberals, but also by their own adversaries, the oligarchs or godos: that the great movement known in our annals by the name Liberal Party was the exclusive work of only one man, Antonio Leocadio Guzmán. The theory is set forth as if he could have been a supernatural power, who, as a newspaper propagandist during several years, had the strength to move a whole society and to found a political party. To reserve for Antonio Leocadio Guzmán the title of Founder of the Liberal

---

[12] Antonio Leocadio Guzmán, *Editoriales de El Venezolano*, I, 3–18.

Party is a simple absurdity. When, for purely personal reasons, Antonio Leocadio separated from Páez's government in 1840, the Liberal Party had already formed the necessities, interests, passions, and principles proclaimed by the doctrine of liberalism and sanctioned by abstract constitutionalism since 1811.[13]

Whether or not Antonio Leocadio Guzmán was the founder of the Liberal Party, he did crystallize the party platform. It has been said of him that he:

. . . founded the popular press. Scarcely erudite in arts and letters, disdaining to look for words or carve sentences, extremely negligent and careless in his style, impatient to say what he wanted to express without regard to form, he liked the "free" pen. He was an abundant and facile improviser. More an orator than a writer, he knew how to popularize the rudiments of government and politics, to enliven the growing instinct for democracy, open new horizons to the masses, and paint the rough landscapes of liberty and salvation. His popularity rapidly increased and left deep roots. Although he had been easily swayed in other periods of his life, he remained tenacious in his determination as a propagandist. Before 1840 he was a supporter of the conservative oligarchy. In 1849 he was the defender of the system of liberal oligarchy. Although on occasions, after 1870, he was the inspirer of systems of autocracy, he was, nevertheless, from 1840 to 1846, the enthusiastic herald and exponent of democratic right.[14]

President Soublette, who succeeded Páez in 1843, believed in the complete freedom of the press to the extent of allowing the quarrels which Antonio Leocadio had with other papers to continue freely. However, when a poem slandering the administration appeared in *El Venezolano*, Antonio Leocadio, as its editor, was held responsible and brought to trial. While the jury was deliberating the extent of his guilt, the liberals took matters into their own hands and, before

---

[13] *Disgregación e integración*, pp. 28–29.
[14] *Ibid.*

any legitimate verdict was rendered, Antonio Leocadio was carried out of the courtroom on the shoulders of the people. This was a personal triumph for him, and February 9, 1844, the day on which this incident occurred, also became a red-letter day in the calendar of the Liberal Party.[15] Leocadio Guzmán was now somewhat of a popular idol. He felt the ground well prepared for his entering the presidential elections in 1847 and said that the mission of *El Venezolano* was complete.

The conservatives nervously watched Antonio Leocadio's popularity grow, and even the moderate liberals were afraid of his radicalism. The constitution gave suffrage only to proprietors, bondholders, and employees, so that the real electors were the richest and most educated, who, in general, mistrusted the Guzmanists. They feared such radical ideas as immediate emancipation of the slaves without compensation to the masters, which was advocated by Leocadio Guzmán.

With the elections approaching, Páez's prestige remained strong enough to make him the most powerful elector, and Guzmán apparently sought his support at the last minute.[16] However, the historian Gil Fortoul says:

Páez, badly advised, instead of recommending Salom or Blanco or another man of conciliatory tendencies, lost his head and did something that meant total eclipse of his own prestige and ten years of bad government for the republic, with five more years of civil war. He recommended the candidacy of Monagas.[17]

The interview which Guzmán was supposed to have with Páez did not materialize and Guzmán's enemies, led by the same Quintero who forced his resignation from the government in 1840, made attempts to implicate him in the unsuccessful revolt against the government led by the Indian

[15] Villanueva, *Vida del valiente ciudadano general Ezequiel Zamora*, p. 58.
[16] *Ibid.*, p. 85.
[17] *Historia constitucional de Venezuela*, II, 260.

Francisco José Rangel in 1846.[18] Guzmán was returning from the attempted interview with Páez at La Victoria when he was detained by the authorities at Antimano. He was shortly freed, but the press launched a campaign against him and he went into hiding.

Meanwhile, with Páez's support and with no formidable candidates against him, José Tadeo Monagas was elected president by the conservative majority. Little did the conservatives realize that their election of Monagas and their continued persecution of Leocadio Guzmán would boomerang against them the very next year.

The case against Antonio Leocadio Guzmán, who was arrested and detained incommunicado in Caracas in October, 1846, was continued through the election campaign. He was constantly questioned about his activities in the Liberal Party, about the money his press made, about his trip to La Victoria, and, since a determined attempt was being made to convict him of conspiracy, particularly about his activities against the government.

On March 21, 1847, Antonio Leocadio Guzmán was found guilty on the charge of conspiracy and attempt to overthrow the government and was sentenced to death, a mandatory penalty in such cases. While Leocadio Guzmán was in jail awaiting the execution of his sentence, his wife, accompanied by young Antonio Guzmán Blanco, went to the home of President Monagas to beg him to spare the life of her husband. Moved by her plea, Monagas lifted her to her feet, saying, "Señora, get up and be assured that I did not come to this place to serve as an instrument of anyone's passions." As a consequence, on June 1, 1847, Monagas commuted the sentence and ordered Leocadio Guzmán into exile.[19]

The commutation of the death sentence of Antonio Leo-

---

[18] Villanueva, *Vida del valiente ciudadano general Ezequiel Zamora*, p. 95.
[19] *Ibid.*, p. 95.

cadio Guzmán and his resultant exile played an important part in the subsequent events of the Monagas administration. Dismayed by the commutation of the death sentence and the general practice, instigated by Monagas, of pardoning political prisoners, Dr. Quintero, representing the views of Páez and the oligarchy, began a propaganda campaign in the press against Monagas, insisting that congress should depose him. This attack precipitated an open break between Monagas and Páez. Monagas continued in power, supported by a group of liberals who were followers of Leocadio Guzmán and who were grateful to Monagas for sparing the former's life.[20]

Páez and his group continued to control the oligarchic majority of the congress, and Monagas was fortifying his position by naming new military chiefs and by organizing new battalions of militia in the capital and nearby districts. As the January, 1848, session of congress approached, the conservatives prepared an indictment against Monagas for unlawfully dismissing the governor of Caracas, General Ustariz. Aware of this effort to impeach Monagas, his supporters in both congress and the militia prepared for the opening of congress on January 24, 1848. When congress convened, the chamber of deputies was surrounded by a mob incited by liberal Monagas supporters who threatened the conservative deputies and who broke up the session with the conservatives fleeing for their lives to their homes or to foreign legations. Monagas stepped in, prevented an attack on the conservatives' homes, and persuaded enough conservative members to return for the session next day so as to give constitutional character to the deliberations and make possible the more liberal legislation.[21]

The events of January 24, 1848, introduced a new era in

[20] González Guinán, *Historia contemporánea de Venezuela*, III, 241.
[21] Gil Fortoul, *Historia constitucional de Venezuela*, II, 282–86.

Venezuela known as the period of the Liberal Oligarchy. Monagas broke completely with Páez and the ultra-conservatives and came to depend on a coalition of the moderate conservatives and liberals. In the following ten years, from 1848 to 1858, during the presidencies of Monagas and of his brother José Gregorio Monagas, a number of important changes were made in the national legislation. The death penalty was abolished for political crimes.[22] The law pertaining to the liberty of contracts, which provided for such drastic punishment of defaulting debtors, was amended. It now provided for auction sales of mortgaged properties, but stipulated that the price arrived at in the auction sale be not lower than half of the actual value of the goods offered at such sales. Furthermore, it was ordered that recognized experts should attend such auction sales and appraise goods offered so that a reasonable and just price could be established for them. The interest rate was fixed at between five and a maximum of nine percent per annum, with the lower figure being the recognized basis in the absence of a contract allowing the higher rate. It was also ordered that no interest could be collected on amounts due as interest. The Liberal Oligarchy considered necessary the intervention of the state to remedy abuse and exploitation and to protect the liberty of individuals incapable of contracting for themselves.[23] The crowning glory of the administrations of the two Monagases was the law abolishing slavery, which was adopted on March 24, 1854, about a decade before the Civil War in the United States achieved the same purpose.[24]

The elder Monagas was ably supported by Leocadio Guzmán during the first years of the new era, but this alliance did not last long. Leocadio Guzmán had presidential aspira-

[22] *Recopilación de leyes*, I, 495.
[23] *Ibid.*, II, 475.
[24] *Ibid.*, III, 149–50.

tions that suffered no discouragement from the fact that his record contained a death sentence, commutation, and exile. He wanted to succeed José Tadeo Monagas, who, while acknowledging Leocadio Guzmán's services to the Liberal Party by allowing him to return from exile and by appointing him first Minister of Interior and later Vice President, did not favor Guzmán's presidential aspirations. The conservatives under Páez did not accept quietly their defeat in January, 1848. That very same year, the following year, and on several other occasions in subsequent years they provoked, under the leadership of Páez, uprisings against the Monagas regime which Monagas was forced to put down with great severity since they endangered his attempts to liberalize Venezuelan politics and the economic structure.[25]

In the course of these conflicts, being distrustful of the conservatives, whose real allegiance was to Páez, and of the liberals, because of their devotion to Leocadio Guzmán, Monagas came to depend more and more on his own council and on that of his immediate personal friends. The element of personalism crept into his administration and became ever stronger in the face of conservative attacks and Leocadio Guzmán's undisguised presidential ambitions. He, therefore, decided to recommend as his successor his brother, José Gregorio Monagas, who was elected in 1851.[26]

Gregorio Monagas's regime, as we have indicated before, had the distinction of abolishing slavery in Venezuela, but it accomplished little else because of the concerted opposition of the Páez oligarchy. To counteract it in a more effective way, José Tadeo resumed the presidency after his brother's term expired in 1855.

By this time, not only the conservative oligarchy, but the

[25] Villanueva, *Vida del valiente ciudadano general Ezequiel Zamora*, pp. 234–37.
[26] Gil Fortoul, *Historia constitucional de Venezuela*, III, 42.

Leocadio Guzmán-led liberals opposed him. The serious charges of attempts at self-perpetuation in office and of personalism were leveled against him. These charges were based on the changes which he brought about in the constitution in March of 1856, when the term of the presidency was changed to six years, the provision against succession in presidential office was eliminated, and centralization of power in the hands of the executive was achieved by limitations imposed on the provincial governments and by increasing the army from three thousand to ten thousand soldiers (used to control the country). Both conservatives and liberals combined in a revolutionary movement against him. Conservative leaders such as Tovar and Toro joined with liberal leaders such as Leocadio Guzmán and the president's own brother, José Gregorio Monagas, in inciting a revolution against him. At the head of this movement against Monagas they placed a liberal, Julián Castro, the governor of the state of Carabobo. Monagas could not stand up to this real and very effective coalition of conservatives and liberals. He was forced to resign the presidency on March 15, 1858, and a coalition government headed by Julián Castro took over the government.[27]

This coalition did not last very long, however. Although at the Valencia Convention, convoked by Castro in 1858, conservatives and liberals cooperated in restoring the four-year presidential period and the principle of presidential rotation, a break in the coalition was imminent. The conservative members of Castro's ministry, primarily concerned with regaining the economic control which the conservative oligarchy held over Venezuela prior to 1848, instituted repressive measures against all those who had taken advantage of the change in legislation pertaining to liberty of contract and had defaults on their debts and obligations assumed prior to 1848. They comprised a large sector of the population

[27] Gil Fortoul, *Historia constitucional de Venezuela*, III, 88.

among the smaller tradesmen, artisans, laborers, and other employees, and the reprisals against them brought forth the resentment and antagonism from the masses against the government. This step provoked great dissension in the two parties supporting Castro, and the liberals, finding that they would not have enough influence with him, broke with his government and abandoned his cabinet. This move on the part of the liberals gave the opportunity to the conservatives to demand and obtain from Castro greater representation in the cabinet and great influence over the policies of the government. The conservatives had little faith in him because of his past as a liberal and because he was favorable to the new issue raised by the liberals—that of federation. Therefore, when the Federal War broke out, the office was taken over by the conservative vice president, Manuel Tovar, who remained in office until General Páez, who was called in to head the government's army against the federalists, took over the government by a *coup d'état* in September of 1861 and established himself as dictator of Venezuela.

The Federal War, when it broke out in the state of Coro on February 20, 1859, brought to a head the continuous unrest and discord which reigned over the country for thirty years. In one respect the war represented the result of the historical divisiveness of Venezuela, the traditions and systems inherited from the organization of the indigenous tribes, from the political and social structure prevalent during the colonial times, and from the economic isolation to which the various groups of the population were subjected by barriers placed by the Spanish fiscal policy which prohibited free communication between provinces and between capital cities. In another respect it was a result of the geography of Venezuela, which divided the country into four distinctly separate sections: the coastal sector along the Atlantic, the northwest section around the lake of Maracaibo, the central

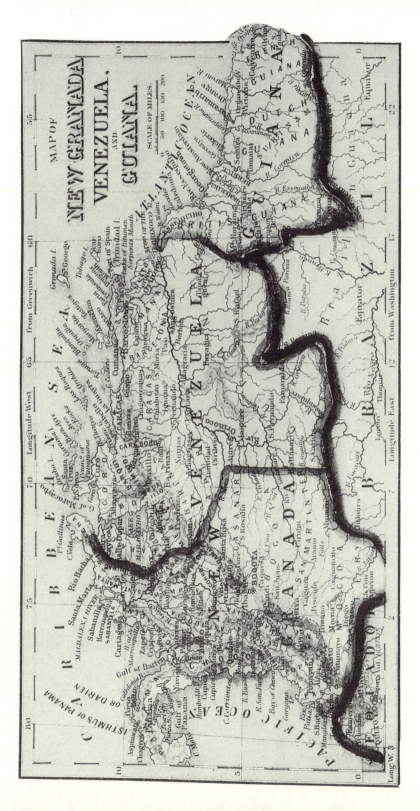

section of the llanos, and the highland section of the Gua-
yanas. Physical obstacles and lack of communication facilities
were responsible for a spirit of regionalism which did not
allow for the creation of any national consciousness or for
the integration and ideals of the people.

On top of these constant forces influencing the political
situation in Venezuela and provoking disunity and strife,
there arose during the rule of the conservative oligarchy
new expressions of class conflict. These were in evidence
during the Civil War of Independence, but they took on new
forms as the new nation strove to find itself. Among the manifestations of the class conflicts were the poverty and the
demoralization of the people; the tyranny exercised by a
military class which rose during the wars and fought for its
privileges; the oppression of the economic laws designed to
protect the wealthy classes and the excesses committed in
their name; the banditry of the llaneros and the penal laws
opposed to the concepts of justice inherent in the pastoral
population; and the persecution and reenslavement of slaves
emancipated during the war but recaptured, in spite of any
rank or honor they might have won in battle.

There were many victims of these conditions. The urban
population, hemmed in by the economic interest of the
wealthy middle class, burdened by ruinous rates of interest,
and deprived of their personal belongings by the operation
of the government credit laws; the military, who were being
dispossessed of their special privileges and who became
economically destitute; the population of the llanos who, ever
since independence and even prior to it, came to depend for
their livelihood on cattle stealing and pillage of richer states
and were now being punished by the noose; slaves returned
to abject slavery by their masters—all these formed social
groups who were unable to conceive the real causes of their
precarious and unhappy existence. Harboring a deep sense

of resentment and hatred toward the government, they were ready to accept as saviors those who held out a promise of protection from government interference and of improvement in their economic conditions.

These were the classes that responded and took up arms in the cause of the Federal War when it was proclaimed in 1859. They were neither cognizant of nor concerned with philosophical definitions and programmatic differences, but they did respond to leaders who spoke of equality and of liberty, who promised the abolition of slavery and of the death penalty, and who carried the assurance of economic improvement and equitable distribution of the national wealth. If this meant in addition a change in the structure of government, the restoration of the autonomy of the individual states, and the replacement of the rulers oligarchically imposed by the men freely elected by the states, it was even more acceptable to the classes. Leocadio Guzmán showed how the leaders played cynically with this resentment when he stated in 1867:

I don't know where the impression that the people of Venezuela have lived for the federation comes from, for they do not know what this word is or what it means. This idea came from me and from others who said, "Assuming that every revolution needs a banner and since the convention of Valencia did not want to baptize the constitution as federal, let us invoke the idea; but if others had said federation, we would have used centralism." [28]

When the issue of federation against centralism was joined with the outbreak in Coro, the leadership of both opposing camps consisted of the following personalities. The conservative camp was led first by General Castro, then by Vice President Manuel Tovar and finally, by a dictator, José Antonio Páez and his secretary general, Pedro Rojas. We

[28] Antonio Leocadio Guzmán, *Documentos históricos sud americanos*, II, 179, as quoted by Vallenilla Lanz, *Cesarismo democrático*.

have in a previous section given an account of the rise to power and of the personality of Julián Castro. As a liberal, he was drafted to lead the liberal-conservative coalition against Monagas. Disowned by the liberals when he gave in to the conservative demands for the restoration of economic restrictive measures, he gradually lost prestige with the conservatives and was supplanted by Vice President Manuel Tovar.

Manuel Tovar, a descendant of the Marqués de Tovar, one of the leading representatives of colonial creole aristocracy, was a representative of the views of the conservative oligarchy which ruled Venezuela prior to Monagas. During his term the discriminatory economic legislation was reintroduced and severe reprisals for past transgressions were instituted by the government. Tovar was concerned primarily with reestablishing the previous economic structure. He had no understanding or sympathy for the spirit of revolt which was sweeping the country. Neither did he have the administrative experience or military prestige to head the government army against the federals. He found it necessary to recall old General Páez and entrust him with the leadership of the army while he attempted to retain administrative control. This division of functions, however, did not work out satisfactorily. Tovar was removed from office by a *coup d'état* in September of 1861 and the leadership of the government and of the country was assumed by General Páez as supreme dictator.

General Páez, at the time that he took over the dictatorship in 1861, was at the culmination of a long career in the service of the country and in the leadership of the army. A native of the llanos, a courageous and forceful leader, he succeeded during the wars of independence in winning the llaneros away from Boves and enlisting their forces in the cause of independence. He proved himself a great military leader who had the confidence and devotion of his men. Politically, he belonged to the conservative group and had at one time contemplated establishing a monarchy, instead of the Federation of Gran Colombia, headed by Bolívar as emperor. When Bolívar rejected this proposal, Páez organized and led a separatist movement which terminated in the withdrawal of Venezuela from the Colombian federation and the proclamation of Venezuela as an independent state in 1830.

Since the liberals were supporters of Bolívar, Páez, upon assuming supreme power in the independent Venezuela, came to depend on the collaboration and on the guidance of the conservative middle class. Thus it turned out that the descendant of the llaneros became head of the conservative oligarchy and the protector of their interests until the Monagas revolt in 1848. When the Federal War broke out in 1859 and the conservatives needed a military leader of known repute and ability, they again turned to Páez who accepted first the command of the army and then proclaimed himself supreme dictator of the country. Páez did not realize the change in the social structure and in the political relations in Venezuela. In the Federal War he depended on allies who were neither astute statesmen nor courageous military leaders. His own ability and personal prestige did not suffice to contain the outbreak of general indignation against the conservatives and the military strength acquired by them. His long hold over Venezuela terminated in the defeat suffered at the hands of the federals when he was forced to agree to the Treaty of Coche and give up his leadership in June, 1863.[29]

Of importance in the Páez dictatorship and in the final stages of the Federal War was the personality of Páez's secretary general, Dr. Pedro José Rojas. An astute politician and a man of definite opportunistic tendencies and personal ambitions, Rojas utilized the years of the Páez dictatorship when

[29] Source: General José Antonio Páez, *Autobiografía*.

he was secretary general to enrich himself through negotiating and handling the fiscal matters of the dictatorship. Toward the end of the Federal War he became convinced of the inevitable defeat of the Páez dictatorship and his only concern was to salvage his personal position and to protect those financial obligations he had assumed on behalf of the dictatorship which provided for continuous, sizable returns to him. It was because of these interests that he welcomed the peace feelers which came from the federal side. In 1863 he persuaded Páez to accept the peace terms proposed at Coche. These terms were arranged by him and a rising opportunist in the federal camp, Antonio Guzmán Blanco.

In the federal camp, in addition to Guzmán Blanco, there figured Leocadio Guzmán, General Juan Falcón, and General Ezequiel Zamora. As has been seen, Antonio Leocadio Guzmán was an experienced politician, a brilliant journalist, and a man of great personal ambition. He became the apostle and the interpreter of the federation ideas and remained throughout the war, as well as for many years after the Federal War, the spokesman for the liberal and federal parties.

The official head of the federalist movement was Juan C. Falcón. The son of wealthy landowners in the state of Coro, he was given a good education in his early youth and also studied in the national college in Coro, where he completed a course in philosophy. He showed great interest in books and was an avid reader of both Spanish and French works. He was pictured as a studious young man of a friendly and peaceful disposition, of great integrity of character, and of unquestionable loyalty. Born in 1820, he was 26 years old during the upheavals of 1846 and 1847, when he became affiliated with the Liberal Party.

With the advent of Monagas, Falcón took greater interest in public affairs and in 1848 was made commandant of the local militia. He applied his industry and his efforts to his post in the army and saw successive promotions, first to a brigadier-general and then to the highest rank in the Venezuelan Army, that of division general.

Politically, Falcón remained a liberal, faithful to the platform of the party as originally propounded by Leocadio Guzmán and Monagas in the early 1850s. In only one aspect did he go further than the Liberal Party platform of those days. He was sincerely convinced that a federal system would be beneficial for Venezuela and advocated this principle within the framework of legal constitutional changes. Although dismayed by the autocratic personalism of Monagas in the latter years of the Monagas dynasty, he remained loyal to Monagas, who gave him his commission, and refused either to head or to join the coalition movement against Monagas in 1858.

When Monagas resigned in March of 1858 and General Castro assumed power, Falcón, with many other liberals, was exiled from Venezuela. Considering himself freed from his duties to both Monagas and Castro, he began to make plans while in exile to organize a movement against the Castro government, which at that time had become dominated by the conservative oligarchy. Basically, he was opposed to war and to bloodshed and was planning a campaign which he hoped would achieve a change in government and the acceptance of the federal principles without extended warfare. His hand, however, was forced by the uprising of General Zamora in Coro on February 20, 1859, and Falcón accepted the leadership of the federal cause and the designation of supreme chief of the federal forces.

Throughout the federal campaign, he attempted to keep his troops from committing excesses against the civil population and from unnecessary bloodshed in battle. Both at the battle of Santa Inés, which represented a federal victory, and in defeat at Coplé, he was impressing his humanitarian and conciliatory tendencies on his troops. Apparently disturbed by the extent of the warfare and the ruin it was bringing upon Venezuela, he sought to bring the war to an early end by attempting to negotiate with the Páez dictatorship. When he was rebuffed in his efforts, he assumed the office of provisional head of the federation, leaving military matters in the hands of his generals and of Antonio Guzmán Blanco. Because of his mild and pacifist attitude, he lost considerable control over the military chieftains and had to depend, in the last period of the war, on Antonio Guzmán Blanco to keep control over the army leaders and to direct the military operations. Although he displayed a great amount of personal vanity, his tendency to delegate his power to others was evident throughout his leadership of the Federal War and while he was at the head of Venezuela after the ultimate victory of the federal cause.[30]

Of a completely different character and inclination was General Ezequiel Zamora, a true liberal, but primarily a dashing warrior who loved wars and battles and was, therefore, at constant odds with Falcón. Zamora was a native of the village of Cura in the province of Caracas. He came from a family of moderate means, acquired the general education common in those days, and became engaged in the trade of hides. Because of the economic discrimination he felt under the conservative oligarchy, he embraced the liberalism expounded by Leocadio Guzmán and after 1840 was one of his ardent supporters. He worked incessantly to further Leocadio Guzmán's candidacy for the presidency in 1846, and when his idol was jailed, he joined the insurrection led by the Indian, Rangel, and for over a year carried on, first an open fight and later guerrilla warfare against the oligarchic government.

Impulsive, reckless, and of unquestionable courage and

[30] Source: Jacinto R. Pachano, *Biografía del Mariscal Juan C. Falcón.*

great military ability, Zamora held off for a year the government forces sent against him. Forced to flee from the province of Caracas, he moved to the north to the Sierra where he acquired complete knowledge of that section of the country and gained many friends and adherents among the population, which contacts he used many years later in winning for the federal cause the population of that section.

Outnumbered by government forces, subdued, and seriously wounded, Zamora was jailed and sentenced to death. He was saved from execution by the general policy of pardon adopted by Monagas. His sentence was commuted to ten years imprisonment, but he soon escaped from jail and was hiding out in Caracas until the events of January, 1848. At that moment, when Monagas broke with the oligarchy, Zamora came out of hiding, offered his services to Monagas, and was named one of the commanders of the militia. Serving under Monagas, he found occasion to revenge himself on his former conservative enemies and was in the thick of fighting against them in their unsuccessful uprisings against Monagas in 1848, 1849, and 1851.

During his army career he served in various provinces, such as Maracaibo, Barcelona, Cumaná, and Coro. While in Coro serving under General Falcón, he met and married the latter's sister, and remained in the state of Coro. There he also came to know and embrace the tendencies towards federation expounded by Falcón. When the leader was exiled by Castro, Zamora, aware of Falcón's plans for a revolutionary movement to bring about the federal system, did not wait for the planned conciliatory action of his brother-in-law. He proclaimed the establishment of the federation on February 20, 1859, and precipitated the fighting which was to last for four years. His impulsive and belligerent character brought him into many conflicts with the commander in chief, Juan Falcón. These conflicts sometimes threatened the solidarity of the federal forces, but Zamora persisted in his ruthless prosecution of the war until he fell at San Carlos on January 10, 1861.[31] The other leader of importance in the Federal War was Antonio Guzmán Blanco, the son of Leocadio Guzmán. Born in 1830, while his father was a trusted member of the Páez administration, young Antonio received the education suitable to children of high officials. He attended the college of Montenegro, admittedly an excellent educational institution. Later, he began to study medicine, but switched to law, receiving his degree at the age of twenty-three. As the son of the "stormy petrel" of Venezuelan politics, young Antonio came to know the glories and vicissitudes of a political career during his early life. When his father was under sentence of death in 1847, he went with his mother to the home of President Monagas to plead for his father's life and accompanied him when his sentence was commuted and he was exiled.

When his father returned to power about a year later, young Antonio enjoyed the opportunities that were offered to the son of a vice president in the Monagas regime. Having completed his legal studies, he entered the foreign service and spent several years in the United States, first at the New York Consulate and later at the Embassy in Washington. He returned to Venezuela at the time when his father broke with Monagas in the 1850s and joined the latter in his political activities in the Liberal Party.

When Juan Falcón was exiled in 1859, young Antonio Guzmán Blanco, also among the proscribed liberals, left with him. This proved the turning point in his career and paved his way to ultimate power in Venezuela. He attached himself to Falcón, who liked this well-educated, versatile, and

[31] Source: Villanueva, *Vida del valiente ciudadano general Ezequiel Zamora.*

accommodating young man, and soon discovered Falcón's personal vanity and exploited this weakness for his own advancement.

Upon returning to Venezuela, while an auditor with Falcón's staff, Guzmán Blanco began to publish a newspaper called *Eco del Ejército* (*Echo of the Army*) in which he extolled Falcón's ideals and personal qualities. Becoming aware of the conflict between Falcón and Zamora, he soon made himself indispensable to both as mediator and as conciliator. While Falcón came to depend on Antonio Guzmán as the secretary general of his provisional government, Guzmán also won over Zamora, who was impressed by this young aristocrat from Caracas who admired his military genius and achievements.

Realizing that a military career was the necessary vehicle for success, Antonio Guzmán, with the support of both Falcón and Zamora, moved from a purely civilian position in the provisional government to a military post in the army. He showed great perception and strategic ability and, after the battle of Salina Cruz, was named a commandant, thus opening the road to his further promotion to the rank of general. When Falcón could not cope with the military chiefs, he delegated military authority to Antonio Guzmán Blanco, who successfully reestablished central control over the army and won the allegiance and the respect of the leading military caudillos commanding the armies of the federation.

Guzmán Blanco, however, was no more interested in the continuation of a bloody war than Falcón was. Having achieved military prominence, he began to investigate ways and means to terminate the war. Inasmuch as the conservative dictatorship had suffered several serious defeats, his approaches to the Páez-Rojas regime were favorably considered.

The secretary general of the Páez government, Rojas, was

favorable to the idea of peace. At his suggestion initial gestures for the peace treaty were begun by Guzmán Blanco. He proposed a conference to be held midway between Caracas and the federal camps. Rojas accepted the proposal and fixed the date for April 23, 1863. The meeting was held at the Coche farm, eight kilometers from Caracas. The Treaty of Coche was signed on May 22, 1863, and put an end to five years of war.

The Treaty of Coche was a very important episode in Guzmán Blanco's political life. There are two interpretations of this treaty. Those who support Guzmán Blanco consider the Treaty of Coche an evidence of his patriotism. They admit that the dictatorship under Páez was almost beaten and that Páez had only several thousand people left who could have been overcome by the combined armies of the west and center. The continuation of the war until complete surrender of Páez, however, would have resulted, according to the partisans of Guzmán Blanco, in certain grave consequences. First, it would have meant continuing warfare in a country already ruined by five years of war. Assuming that final victory was on the side of the federalists, the dispersed forces of the dictator government would have continued in a guerrilla phase, much as the federal forces after the debacle of Coplé, and would have kept the country in constant turmoil. The second reason given by the partisans of Guzmán Blanco was that if Caracas were to be taken by force, a sanguinary battle would have resulted which would have demolished the city, killed many people, and made the union of the various struggling groups impossible. Thirdly, these partisans felt that although Páez had been discredited by the last years of the Federal War, he still commanded a large following in the country because of his previous accomplishments as the founder and organizer of Venezuela, and that he would have had many supporters in the country among the caudillos. This would have kept the country in continuous turmoil.

Setting himself against the federals, who wanted a military triumph, Guzmán Blanco exposed himself to attacks from many of the federal generals, and even seriously jeopardized his position with Falcón, who did not like some of the provisions of the original treaty negotiated at Coche between Guzmán Blanco and Rojas. Those who opposed Guzmán Blanco saw in the Treaty of Coche a deliberate bid on his part for personal advancement and glory. Level de Goda, who is one of the main authorities on the military campaigns (in which he also participated), claims that Guzmán Blanco precipitated the treaty in order to gain by political means and diplomacy the prestige which would not otherwise have come to him for military reasons. He considers this move on the part of Guzmán Blanco a master stroke which established him in the eyes of the country as a man of reason, firmness, and peace and made secure his position in the forthcoming government of the federation, despite the fact that he did not contribute militarily to its success.

At the same time, however, the treaty exposed Guzmán to the criticism voiced by many of his opponents that his agreement with Rojas was a deal for the sake of advancing him financially. It was claimed that Rojas showed to Guzmán the details and potentialities of the pending loans and that Guzmán was influenced by the prospects of acquiring great wealth.

This controversy demonstrates that Guzmán Blanco emerged upon the political scene under the same cloud of suspicion which was to cast its shadow over his entire career, as will become increasingly evident in the following chapters where his rise to undisputed power and his rule over Venezuela are discussed. At this point, it should be noted that the conflicts and dissonance in Venezuelan society were such as to make ideological agreement and social solidarity extremely difficult. The four-year Federal War illustrates the basic difficulties. The only means by which national political order could be restored was through a strong personal leader, but under the circumstances such a leader was bound to placate irreconcilable interests and could hardly achieve perfect sincerity on all sides. Guzmán Blanco, by his character and training, seemed to answer a political need. He was the national caudillo.

CHAPTER IV

THE BROKEN ROAD TO POWER

THE END OF THE FOUR-YEAR FEDERAL WAR in 1863 left the country in a weak condition, especially since the previous fifty years had themselves seen almost constant conflict in the form of wars, revolutions, and political instability. The country was in a destitute situation financially; the old isolation and divisiveness was still present; and the Federal War had not fully solved the basic issue over which it was fought, the struggle for power between the conservative-centralist faction and the liberal-federalist element. Any leader who took over at this juncture and remained in power for an extended period would have somehow to solve at least some of the problems facing the nation. At the same time he would have to use other means as well—those associated with political skill of an often ruthless and self-interested character—to stay in power.

Beginning shortly after the end of the Federal War, Guzmán Blanco presided over the destiny of Venezuela for about a quarter of a century (if we include both his service in the Falcón government and his own presidential terms). He achieved this feat by meeting the two kinds of necessities which faced him. He played an important role in rebuilding the country—by consolidating its political structure, by integrating it through development of communications and transportation, by stabilizing its agriculture and commerce, and by giving impetus to education and eliminating the social control of the Church to a large extent. At the same time, he looked after his personal interests by making himself independently wealthy, by treating others as instrumentalities, and by violating the very laws of his own constitution. In a sense, under the conditions of the times, the second aspect of his career was necessary for the first. At least it would seem that the country desperately needed political continuity and strength and that a caudillo was the only kind of political figure who could supply it.

In order to demonstrate the two sides of the caudillo regime, the present chapter and the next two will be devoted to a biography of Guzmán Blanco during his twenty-five years of dominance in the country. They will show his great organizing ability as a civil administrator and his acumen and craftiness as a politician. They will show his capacity to solve enough of the country's problems and enough of his political problems to stay in power. Later periods in the history of the republic may show that politics could be less ruthless, but the caudillo formula for the moment had a certain functional relationship to the situation of Venezuela between 1864 and 1888. Indeed, the bases of caudillo rule were not extinguished when Guzmán's rule was over. The foundations laid by him were not sound enough for that.

The victory of the federals under the leadership of Falcón and Guzmán Blanco, the signing of the Treaty of Coche negotiated by Guzmán Blanco, and the elevation of Falcón to the provisional presidency with Guzmán as vice president, in July, 1863, projected the latter into a leading role in the new government of the country. From 1863 to 1867, while Falcón was nominally president, Guzmán Blanco was in actual command of the country, except for the time that he spent in Europe negotiating loans. During these four years he succeeded, through adroit financial maneuvers, in amassing a large personal fortune. He also succeeded in acquiring the reputation of an efficient administrator, able to cope with the problems of the government and with the maintenance of internal order in the country. Because his power stemmed from the authority delegated to him by Falcón and his position was dependent on the good will of Falcón, he continued to profess the liberalist and federalist ideas of the leader, thus appearing before the country as a man who combined the ideology of the Liberal Party with great personal talents and administrative ability.

There were three tasks to which Guzmán Blanco devoted himself during this period. The first was to consummate the foreign loans which he had planned ever since the Federal War. Second, he was interested in bringing about a constitutional reform which would embody the platform of the Federal Party. Third, taking advantage of Falcón's practice of delegating authority and retiring to his native state of Coro, Guzmán Blanco was anxious to prove to the country that he was a man of ability and of decisive action and thus pave the way for his assumption of presidential powers in his own right and not as either vice president or as temporary substitute for Falcón. He saw to it that arrangements for a foreign loan, which apparently played a role in the negotiations at Coche, were carried out as soon as the federals assumed power. When Falcón became provisional president in July of 1863, he named Antonio Guzmán minister of the treasury and foreign relations. This post gave him the opportunity to carry out his plans for a foreign loan.

Before the federal triumph, Guzmán Blanco had often spoken of the need to contract a loan from a foreign country in order to compensate the federalists in money for their services. After the triumph this theme never escaped his daily conversation, and within two weeks after he became Secretary of the Treasury he managed to obtain from Falcón the necessary authorization for negotiating the loan and left for Europe on August 8, 1863.[1]

[1] Level de Goda, *Historia contemporánea de Venezuela política y militar*, p. 558.

This broad authority was defined in the following instructions explained in the letters which were sent to him on August 6, 1863, by the president of the republic and the members of the cabinet authorizing him

as fiscal deputy of the republic, to contract a loan in London, or some other commercial center in Europe or America, which would not exceed two million pounds sterling, with the most favorable rate of interest and other conditions he could obtain; being able to pledge especially the free part of the imports of the customs house of La Guaira and Puerto Cabello, or the total import rights of the other customs houses of the republic, or even to guarantee any other possessions or national property for the payment of interest and for the amortization of the capital. Besides, General Guzmán Blanco was authorized to receive the price of the loan, arrange for its transfer to Caracas, give receipts, settlements of accounts, sign bonds, settle conditions of payment, delegate authority to whomever he trusted, and invest part or the whole amount of the loan in whatever fiscal operation that might be considered beneficial to the interests of the republic in London and make suitable arrangements for Venezuela with them.[2]

As can be seen from these instructions, Guzmán Blanco was empowered not only to negotiate a loan and to mortgage whatever national resources he considered necessary, but he was also given the discretion of disposing of the proceeds of the loan in the manner that he felt was best. In this way he was given complete control over Venezuela's finances and national economy.

It can be seen that the desperate economic situation of the country and the political atmosphere of the time was conducive to getting foreign capital on terms bad for the country but possibly good for the leaders. In this way the economic independence of many Latin American countries was seriously jeopardized.

[2] González Guinán, *Historia contemporánea de Venezuela*, VIII, 170–73.

Upon his arrival in London, Guzmán Blanco first reviewed the outstanding obligations of Venezuela to English creditors and then began to sound out the financial houses about a loan which would make it possible to liquidate previous indebtedness and consolidate all Venezuelan indebtedness into one large loan. In his efforts he was assisted by Giacomo Servadio, a personal friend and partner of Dr. Pedro Rojas, the man with whom Guzmán Blanco had negotiated the Treaty of Coche. Servadio, who spoke English and who had personal acquaintance with several English banking and investment houses, acted as the go-between for Guzmán and the English financiers.

Having made arrangements for a loan of a million-and-a-half pounds, Guzmán Blanco returned to Venezuela to obtain congressional approval for the loan and to participate in the constitutional convention convoked by Falcón for the purpose of writing a federal constitution.

When Guzmán Blanco arrived in Venezuela, he learned that his plans for the loan were meeting with considerable opposition among the public in general and among the members of the national assembly, which had to approve the loan. Rumors circulating in the country held that the personal interest of Guzmán Blanco was the dominant motivation for the loan. These rumors were inspired by the fact that he precipitated his departure for England to negotiate the loan within two weeks after his appointment to the ministry of the treasury, as well as by the fact that he used in London the services of Giacomo Servadio, who was known to be the personal representative of former Secretary General Rojas of the Páez dictatorship. The latter fact renewed the charges leveled at Guzmán at the time of the Coche treaty, that of a secret agreement between the federal government and the Páez-Rojas dictatorship, and led to attacks on the loan negotiations.

The vice president, however, was not dismayed by this concerted opposition. He first used his personal influence with Falcón to obtain the latter's approval of the loan. Then, while Falcón stayed away from Caracas during the sessions of the national assembly, Guzmán and his father, Leocadio Guzmán, both of them deputies of the assembly, conducted an intensive drive among the members of the assembly to win their support. The persuasive eloquence of the two Guzmáns and the fact that Antonio Guzmán assumed again the post of minister of the treasury and held the purse strings of the country in his hands, influenced many members of the congress to support him. When the plans for the loan came to a vote, they were approved by a large majority, and Falcón, acting on the strength of this approval, gave Guzmán Blanco full power in February of 1864 to consummate the loan.[3]

The assembly which considered the matter of the loan was also the constitutional assembly which wrote the federal Constitution of 1864. It thus gave Guzmán Blanco the opportunity to accomplish his second objective. This constitution incorporated the aspirations of the federalist movement. Since Guzmán claimed in years to come that he was responsible in a large measure for the formulation of this constitution, even though he was away in London at the time the constitution was passed, we are giving here the basic sections of this document.

1. The federal system in Venezuela was to be reestablished and the country divided into twenty states, a federal district, and territories of Coagira and Amazonas.

2. The congress was to consist of two houses, a chamber of deputies elected directly by the people and a senate elected by the legislatures of the states.

[3] *Recopilación de leyes*, IV, 298.

3. The president of the republic was to be elected every four years through a direct and secret vote. Two designates for vice president were also to be elected to serve if the president should be unable to discharge his duties.

4. A federal supreme court was established whose members were to be elected from among candidates submitted by the legislatures of the states.

5. The death penalty was abolished under all circumstances.

6. Universal male suffrage was provided in the constitution, the only limitation being minority of age.

7. Complete liberty of the press was guaranteed by the constitution.[4]

This constitution differed from the centralist Constitution of 1830 and from the more liberalized Constitution of 1850 in the sense that it definitely established the division of the country in federal autonomous states; that it provided for universal suffrage without any financial requirements or limitations on the part of the electors; that it completely abolished the death penalty in Venezuela; and that it provided for the widest guarantees of personal freedom and freedom of the press.

Although the constitution thus settled on paper the issue of the Federal War, it did not settle it in actuality. The issue came up again and represented one of the major problems in Guzmán's period of power. It rested upon the profound difficulty of a country needing central control but having local and class loyalties of an extreme kind. Guzmán's devotion to the federal principle was by no means complete in practice.

Guzmán Blanco, having promulgated the constitutional reforms pledged by the Federal Party and having concluded

[4] *Constitución de los Estados Unidos de Venezuela.*

the loan negotiations which helped him to amass a great personal fortune, turned now to his third objective, that of establishing his own popularity and leadership in the country. He had been away from Venezuela during most of 1863 and 1864, and during that time the coordination of the army, the local caudillos, and the central government, achieved through Guzmán Blanco's efforts at the close of the Federal War, had become weakened and ofttimes disrupted. Falcón's indecisive attitude with regard to the quarrels of the local chieftains, his dislike of the capital and his practically continuous absence from Caracas, and his delegation of authority to various individuals of conflicting viewpoints and doubtful ability created, on the one hand, a loss of confidence in the federal government and, on the other hand, an opportunity for the defeated conservatives to attempt to regain their power. Instead of presiding over the government in Caracas and pursuing a definite administrative and economic policy, Falcón preferred to lead military expeditions personally against minor uprisings, leaving the government in other hands and thus contributing to continuous political unrest and economic deterioration. Guzmán Blanco was well aware of this situation when he returned to Venezuela in November of 1864, and when Falcón named him to carry out the duties of the presidency, he willingly accepted the designation, in which he saw the chance of his personal advancement.

From November, 1864, to May, 1866, Guzmán Blanco headed the federal government. During that period he concentrated on the pacification of the country through gaining effective control over the local caudillos and through supporting the federal legislatures and presidents. He regularized the fiscal administration of the country by a resolution of the ministry of the treasury which ordered a reduction of unauthorized expenses and demanded an account from each ministry of all operations during the federal administrations. The customs houses at La Guaira and Puerto Cabello were ordered to send daily reports of their income and disbursements. All contracts of the former government except those made by Falcón were ordered canceled and instructions were given for the ministry of the treasury to issue all purchase orders. Further decrees within the treasury department provided for punctual payment of public expenses, which appeased both the army and the public employees, who had not been paid for many months.[5]

During his stay in Europe, Guzmán Blanco had taken particular trouble to stimulate the creation in Caracas of a bank of discount and deposit and to advance the projected work on the central railroad of Venezuela. The railroad was to leave Puerto Cabello and break into two lines at El Paulito, one to continue via the coast to San Felipe and the other to Caracas via Valencia and the valleys of Argus. In the first days of December the man chosen to be director of the bank, as well as the engineers for the railroad, arrived in Caracas from Europe. The day of the bank's installation was fixed for January 1, 1865, and the railroad company was to begin work on December 21, 1864.[6]

Other administrative acts of Guzmán during that period included the organization of the ministry of post offices, the establishment of rules for the examination of the accounts of employees, and the organization of fiscal matters of the federal district and dictation of the law of budget for that district.[7]

In the course of these activities Guzmán Blanco exercised a considerable measure of authority which helped the dissenting elements to bring about a rupture between him

[5] These measures have been put in effect through a number of decrees which were published in the *Recopilación de leyes*, IV, 388, 389, 391, 404.

[6] González Guinán, *Historia contemporánea de Venezuela*, VIII, 363–66.

[7] *Recopilación de leyes*, IV, 426, 437.

and Falcón. Conservatives, aware of the greater danger to their chances of returning to power under Guzmán Blanco, and liberals, concerned over signs of autocracy displayed by him, insinuated to Falcón that the acting president was overstepping the authority granted to him by Falcón and that he was working toward displacing Falcón as the constitutional president of Venezuela. Falcón, who had at that time begun to consider a constitutional change which would make it possible for him to succeed himself in the presidency, saw in Guzmán Blanco's objection to such a change a confirmation of the rumors against him. Falcón returned to Caracas and resumed the presidency. Being aware of the other man's popularity, he did not break with him openly. He first appointed him as chief of the army of the federal district and later on, when their disagreement over the forthcoming election began to be more acute, he sent him on a mission to Europe.

Although he coveted the office of president, Falcón did not like to exercise it. He left Caracas for Coro within a short time, entrusting the government to two of his subordinates, both of whom were inimical to Guzmán. They seized the opportunity to discredit the latter and to change the political administration and economic measures instituted by him. Utilizing the split within the ranks of the leadership of the Federal Party, a split now apparent to all, the conservatives saw their chance of returning to power.

Mindful of the successful coalition of conservatives and liberals which unseated General José Tadeo Monagas in 1858, they now again turned to the idea of a coalition between the revengeful conservatives and the disappointed liberals. As the leader of this coalition they chose the same General Monagas whom they had forced out a decade ago. General Monagas, hoping that his personal intervention would prevent a bloody revolution, acceded to their request to head the revolution, which was called the Blue Revolution because of the color of the flag that they adopted. Falcón, left to his own devices, was easily defeated and forced to flee Venezuela, while Monagas became the head of the country. The conciliatory influence of the elder Monagas, however, did not last long. He died in November of 1868. His place was taken by his nephew, Ruperto Monagas, who was completely under the influence of the conservatives.

While these events were taking place in Venezuela, Guzmán Blanco remained in Paris watching the developments. When it became clear to him that Falcón was definitely eliminated and that his loyalty to Falcón would no longer deter him from seeking the leadership of the Liberal Party, he decided to return to Venezuela. He arrived two months after the triumph of the Blues,[8] in time to serve as an anchor for the reorganizing liberal element. He was determined to try every legal measure to upset the reactionaries before resorting to arms. He thought it advisable to wait and see if the "liberal" elements in the present government would dominate. In this respect he differed greatly from Falcón, who from his exile in Curaçao advocated an unusual course for his mild and peaceful attitude, an armed revolt against the Blues. Guzmán Blanco took an active part in influencing the coming elections by creating a daily paper called *La Unión Liberal*, edited by Vicente Coronado.[9]

The Blue fusion weakened to the breaking point. Most of the men surrounding the government belonged to the Conservative Party, just as most of the liberals in the government remained spectators. The liberals were divided. The smaller group was in accord with the militarist policy of Falcón. The other and larger group, while it did not reject Falcón, aspired

[8] The conservatives were called the Blues because of the color of their flag, while the Liberals were known as the Yellows for the same reason. (Ruiz, *Historia patria*.)

[9] Aldrey, *Rasgos biográficos*, pp. 315–16.

to a position of equality in the government and sustained the regime of General Ruperto Monagas and his candidacy for the presidency. This group believed in the advocacy of peaceful evolution and recognized as its immediate center Guzmán Blanco, professing complete faith in him.

The latter was in those days a great name, a man with a notable past as a statesman as well as a man of considerable wealth, but prejudice of every kind began to be directed against him. Both liberals and conservatives began to place large obstacles in his way.

The agitation against Antonio Guzmán reached its climax on the night of August 14, when a mob incited by government-led orators attacked his home while a great reception to national and foreign dignitaries was being held. For hours the mob stormed the house seeking to break in, with the government forces looking on indifferently. Guzmán and his family were rescued by the American minister, in whose home they remained until Guzmán, accompanied by his father, left Caracas on the 18th. He was informed of the events of the 18th, when his home was attacked for a second time, and on the 31st he wrote a letter to *La Opinión Nacional*,[10] thanking his sympathizers and giving his own account of the outbreak of the 14th.

In Curaçao, Guzmán prepared for war. He was surrounded there by other liberals in exile, including many leading generals. A revolutionary committee was also organized in Caracas. Other committees were set up in other parts of the republic. In Curaçao the old journalist, Antonio Leocadio Guzmán, was publishing some pamphlets called *Evangelio Liberal* which defended the Liberal Party, himself, and General Guzmán Blanco against the charges made from Caracas and by the editor of *El Federalista*.

Hurried mobilization began on both sides. While the gov-

---

[10] González Guinán, *Historia contemporánea de Venezuela*, IX, 274.

ernment depended on its regular army, some conservative elements, and some members of the clergy, the opposing forces appealed again to the same local caudillos and the same class elements which helped them win the Federal War. The response of these elements was an encouraging one. While it was true that the four years of federal government contributed but little to the improvement of political and economic conditions in the country, the Falcón government took the initial steps toward introducing the federal system of government and it did abolish the death penalty, two of the issues which concerned the major part of the country. The local caudillos, most of whom had been for awhile state presidents under the federal constitution, were anxious to protect their newly acquired rights. Out of fear of the conservative reaction, the signs of which had already become noticeable during the short period of the Blue government, the masses followed the local caudillos and the cause of Guzmán Blanco. While fighting continued in several sections until the end of 1871, the victory of the Guzmán-led forces was assured as soon as Guzmán landed in Venezuela on February 14, 1870.

The successful leader was advancing the program for the political and military consolidation of the revolution when the Blue congress met in Caracas. There was still a small minority in congress in favor of peace, but the majority had turned Caracas into a military camp and prepared to meet the liberal forces. Guzmán's progress, however, could not be stopped. After a series of successful encounters, he overcame the defenses of the city and entered Caracas on April 27, 1870, completing the last step which led him to undisputed power in Venezuela for over two decades.

CHAPTER V

THE TIME OF DOMINANCE

THE ENTRY OF GUZMÁN BLANCO into Caracas on April 27, 1870, did not terminate the war against the Blue forces. His victorious march of seventy days from San Felipe to Caracas opened the road to the capital, but the major part of the country remained embroiled in a ruthless war between the federal and Blue forces. Guzmán's capture of the capital represented a symbolic victory for his cause, but the cause was not yet triumphant. This victory had to be implemented with a decisive defeat of his opponents, whom it took two years to finally subdue and pacify.

To assure the country that his forces were victorious and for the purpose of introducing order and providing legitimate authority for his government, General Guzmán Blanco delivered an address on the day when the army of the revolution occupied Caracas. He denied that responsibility for the war lay with him or with his cause. He stated that during his march on Caracas he had offered the Blue government liberal terms of peace which were rejected. Now power was in his hands, but he and his victorious army were only the agents and the temporary instruments of right and justice. Accordingly, by virtue of his new position, he made the following pronouncements and decrees:

1. The states were invited to each elect a plenipotentiary to go to Valencia.

2. Of these plenipotentiaries, one more than half of the total number would suffice to install congress on the next June 15th or as soon thereafter as this quorum could be convened.

3. The first act of the congress would be to convoke popular elections in conformity with the Constitution of 1864.

4. The congress of plenipotentiaries was to elect a provisional president and first and second delegates.

5. All elections, laws, contracts, and decrees promulgated since June 28, 1868, to this day were repudiated by the revolution which Guzmán Blanco headed, and all peace pacts were subject to his approval.

6. The rights of the people (*Derecho de Gentes*), part of the 1864 constitution, would be scrupulously observed.[1]

These decrees were sent the same day to the state presidents. The circular accompanying the decrees reaffirmed the responsibility of the former government in the events that had occurred and also declared that his revolution had, among its various aims, respect for state sovereignty. It urged that the state governments promptly elect plenipotentiaries for the Valencia congress as stipulated.

At the same time, Guzmán Blanco also organized a cabinet consisting of men in whom he had complete personal confidence, including among them his father, to whom he entrusted the very important portfolio of interior and justice, the ministry which had control over the internal security of the country. The appointment of this cabinet was Guzmán's first step toward the assumption of a virtual dictatorship.

While the continuance of the war and the need for strong, decisive action at a time when the country was politically and administratively disorganized may have justified his assumption of the extraordinary prerogatives provided for by the constitution in such emergencies, Guzmán utilized these conditions to entrench himself solidly in power and to retain autocratic control of the government.

[1] *Recopilación de leyes,* V, 3–4.

The congress of state plenipotentiaries, convoked by him in his message of April 27th, met in July of 1870 in Valencia. The fifteen delegates to the congress derived their authority from the presidents of the states, who in turn depended on Guzmán Blanco's confidence. This congress duly elected Guzmán Blanco provisional president of Venezuela, but because of the composition of the congress all decisions had fallen, under the guise of the constitution, into the sole hands of Guzmán Blanco. On July 20, 1870, he took the oath as president of Venezuela, thus formalizing powers which he had already acquired without the need or intention of accounting to anyone in exercising these powers. His word was the law. His administrative acts were swift and decisive. He was uncompromising with his enemies on the battlefield and at home and he demanded absolute obedience from his ministers, military leaders, and partisans.

The first measures dictated by Guzmán after taking Caracas were directed against the lynchers of Santa Rosalia who had attacked his home on August 14, 1869. Another measure ordered the confiscation of the properties and of the capital of the leaders of the Blue government and of their supporters in Caracas and other parts of the republic. These measures were carried out with the greatest severity, the first because of the revengeful spirit of Guzmán and the second because, in addition to punishing his enemies, the confiscation provided the necessary means for the maintenance of his army and his government.

Mindful of the fact that the students of the university of Caracas took an active part in the demonstrations against him during the Blue regime, he undertook the first act of direct interference on the part of the government in the affairs of Caracas university, reorganizing it on the charge that it was a "nest of godos." He thus initiated a process that was finally to destroy altogether the autonomy of that institution.

The university of Mérida was subjected to the same treatment. In fact, both universities were annexed to the party in power, which nominated their personnel and voted their budgets.[2]

To consolidate his position and to discourage dissentient manifestations, he issued several decrees which were designed to allay economic discontent and to increase prosperity. On May 1, 1870, ten days after taking Caracas, he dictated two decrees, one abolishing customs duties on exports and the other reducing by seventy percent the duties which burdened imports. In forty consecutive years since 1830 no improvements had been made in the taxation system. Guzmán Blanco did what his predecessors had not dared to do for four decades.[3]

On May 7th he published another decree designed to popularize him with the masses and to prove that the chief of the revolution was deeply interested in the improvement of their condition. The decree stated that the state was taking over the responsibility for the debts incurred with the masters of peons and day workers who had taken up arms in support of the revolution.[4]

Guzmán Blanco did not remain long in Caracas. Intensive fighting was carried on on many fronts and the war claimed his personal attention. The enemy was still holding out in several states, and Guzmán prepared personally to lead the battle against them. He opened a campaign at Aragua and Carabobo. He arrived in La Victoria and quickly, after assuring peace in Aragua, moved on to Tarmero and Maracay. As he advanced he ordered the seizure of properties in the disaffected areas, authorizing the civil and military chiefs of the

[2] *Recopilación de leyes,* V, 93–94.
[3] *Ibid.,* V, 5–59.
[4] *Ibid.,* V, 63.

states concerned to administer these properties and to apply their revenues to the cost of the war.[5]

At this time Guzmán Blanco was forty-one years of age, in full vigor, and at the height of his physical and intellectual capacities. He was in a superior position to the various leaders who had become famous on the battlefield but who lacked his political and administrative capacities. Some surpassed him in certain aptitudes, but none possessed the balance and the diverse attributes which enabled him to convert himself into the supreme coordinator of all the aspirations and interests that could be harnessed to his ambitions. His natural intelligence had well assimilated the experience of the twelve years he had gone through, at times as an exile, a fighter, one who dealt with cultivated and uncultivated people, a concocter of intrigue, a leader, a European traveller, a man making a fortune by whatever means he could, a man pursued, and finally a man acclaimed and triumphant. His days of armed fighting to defend his future, which forced him to divide his attention between army action and government affairs, had the cumulative effect of shaping his personality into that of a Caesar, the surrogate of an unworkable democracy who was to force his authority on Venezuela for more than eighteen years. It was no longer necessary for him to hide any part of his personality, and he now began to show the character that was to make him an undisputed dictator.

In the field he acted in a firm and decisive way. His instructions to his ministers and to his commanders were well organized and his strategy for the campaign against the conservatives was well planned and efficiently executed. Valencia fell on the 15th of May, and his next campaign was directed against Puerto Cabello. In a communication to his ministers Guzmán Blanco announced that Valencia would

[5] *Ibid.*, V, 64–5.

suffer nothing from the army and that Puerto Cabello must now choose between the misfortunes that befell the forced occupation of Caracas and the respect for all rights that was enjoyed by the peaceably possessed Valencia.[6]

Puerto Cabello surrendered on May 18th. The Guzmán forces could not be stopped and the conservatives decided to withdraw and carry the war on in the east and the west. Guzmán organized the newly occupied territory, appointing a military chief for the state of Carabobo and dispatching his generals to clean out the remaining guerrilla fighters in the state. Recognizing that the next attack from the conservatives would come through the means of a maritime expedition, he began a return trip to Caracas in order to organize a fleet to send against the conservatives.

While he was in campaign outside the capital, Guzmán initiated a correspondence with his ministers. This correspondence was compiled by *La Opinión Nacional* in 1875 in a volume entitled *Memorandum del General Guzmán Blanco*. The letters appearing in the *Memorandum* are interesting and instructive for their demonstration of the character of their author. The writing reveals great capacity for detail, a masterful grasp of all matters of state handled by the various ministries, and an autocratic and, at times, insolent attitude toward his ministers. On one occasion, when he was displeased with the excessive expenditures on the part of his cabinet, he wrote:

I have been away from Caracas ten days with three times the army which I left there, and my expenses have been three times less than those of yours. There is no explanation for this but the lack of firmness in preventing abuse of the situation. Why do you need to spend three thousand pesos daily in Caracas? At that pace everything we are doing is useless. Let him yell who will. And if some want to rise up, let them do it. And if they

---

[6] González Guinán, *Historia contemporánea de Venezuela*, XI, 390–91.

want to ruin their own work this way, let them do it, but the daily expenses of this government should not go over one thousand pesos. If there is a chief, if there are officers who make threats on this account, challenge them to carry out their own threats. In such cases go to your houses and tell me to go to mine, for in a country in which such phenomena occur, it would be dishonorable to serve with healthy intentions.[7]

Letters written on other occasions and quoted in other chapters of this work demonstrate his strong determination to uproot the conservative opposition at any cost and by any means and suggest his drive for absolute and undisputed control of the affairs of Venezuela.

His return to Caracas was followed by receipt of favorable news concerning the progress of the war. San Sebastián, Barcelona, and Maturín had been occupied by his forces and some guerrillas had begun to lay down their arms in Bolívar. He also received news of the incorporation of the state of Guayana into the revolution.

Encouraged by this favorable progress of the war, Guzmán now turned to matters pertaining to the civil administration. On June 27, 1870, he promulgated a decree to establish free and obligatory primary education. Up to this time the national government had only the colleges of secondary instruction under its supervision. Primary instruction was reserved for the provinces and municipalities, who because of small incomes could do little, especially in the unfortunate times since 1846. Consequently, only the few who had means could educate their children. Guzmán Blanco issued his famous decree as based on the following considerations:

That all associates had the right of participation in the outstanding benefits of education; that this was necessary in the republic in order that the army should be assured of the rights of citizens and of the ability to fulfill its duties; that this education should

[7] *Memorandum del General Guzmán Blanco*, p. 27.

be universal and be directed to that which is the basis of all ulterior knowledge and all moral perfection; that under the federal constitution the public power should establish such free primary education; that free and obligatory teaching of general and moral principles was to be established, as well as that of reading and writing the mother language, practical arithmetic, the metric system, and of the federal constitution. Free instruction would further include all the range of human knowledge that the Venezuelans might want to acquire, to be extended gratuitously by the public power insofar as possible.[8]

Every father, mother, tutor, or person entrusted with a child seven years old and under age was required to give him the requisite instruction. If such a person could not undertake the obligation, he was to send the child to a local public school. The nation, states, and municipalities were to do all possible to develop primary gratuitous instruction and to fulfill their own obligations in this respect. The decree created a national direction of primary instruction and contemplated the creation of sectional committees in districts, parochial districts, and neighborhoods and also committees of popular societies to cooperate in the operation of this law. Further, to endow the law with its own income so as to insure its execution, Guzmán Blanco ordered by decree that special revenue stamps should be affixed to all documents. This tax was to begin operating in January, 1871.[9]

Aldrey related that the first school set up in 1871 was named after Guzmán Blanco. The special fund to sustain the program was given such extension that even the people of the most remote regions of Venezuela were affected by the act. Traveling teachers came to these places. Administration of the act was placed under the minister of development to

[8] *Recopilación de leyes*, V, 70 ff.
[9] *Recopilación de leyes*, V, 75.

be carried out by a national direction assisted by state, district, and parochial committees.

The war situation soon again claimed Guzmán's attention. The process of pacification was far from complete. The situation in the west was becoming serious with the convergence of several groups of Blue forces. Guzmán moved his headquarters to Puerto Cabello, from which place he directed personally various military movements and the dispatch of additional troops to contain the enemy forces. His strategy resulted in a decisive triumph of the liberal forces at Guama, but this victory precipitated a conflict with the Catholic Church which continued for many years.

In the course of the war a number of Catholic priests had managed to enlist religious sentiment on one side of the struggle. Not only did they address their sermons to the issue, but some even joined the Blue troops. At the Vatican Council from which Archbishop Guevara had just returned, the condemnation of liberalism by Pope Pius IX also influenced the situation in no small measure, and at the El Guarico battle, the Blue bands were seen with an image of the Virgin of the Rosario.

By amicable negotiations with Archbishop Guevara, Guzmán Blanco had contrived the removal of certain priests, among them the vicar of Valencia, Delgado, of whom Guzmán Blanco said: "He had converted the church of Valencia into a general headquarters of the reactionary oligarchy of the west."

Guzmán succeeded in having him confined in Caracas, just as was the vicar of San Carlos. But soon a new complication arose to produce a real rupture between ecclesiastical authorities and those of the new regime.

After the liberal triumph at Guama, Guzmán Blanco's minister of the interior asked for a *Te Deum* service. Archbishop Guevara refused to oblige on the ground that fratricide should not be celebrated and the Guzmán Blanco government should extend complete political amnesty to the defeated. As a consequence, Guevara was exiled and a serious conflict with the Church was produced.[10] The military successes of the liberals in the subsequent months, in the course of which Coro, Maracaibo, Mérida, and Carabobo were captured or surrendered, seemed, however, to have produced a change of attitude and objectives in the president. On November 1, 1870, he suddenly decided to free twenty-four political prisoners of importance.[11] On November 12 twenty-five more political prisoners were liberated, and on the 26th he liberated a few others and revoked the decree of May 12th which provided for confiscation of enemy property.

About the same time Guzmán Blanco turned to the pressing economic problems of the country. The credit of the country had been ruined by the war and by the continuous military expenses which consumed the income of the government. Holders of government bonds and obligations had not been paid for several years and were pressing the government for the settlement of their claims. For this purpose he organized two companies which attempted to satisfy the creditors and produce additional capital. On November 3rd he organized the Commission of Public Credit, whose function was to bring about the unblocking of capital through the redemption of the public debt, and on December 9, the Company of Credit, whose purpose was to obtain for the government advances on public income and facilitate fiscal operations. A special bond issued and guaranteed by the government found great acceptance among the Venezuelan

[10] Briceño, *Los ilustres,* pp. 107–8.
[11] González Guinán, *Historia contemporánea de Venezuela,* IX, 451.

public.[12] These two measures brought about stability and
rehabilitated the public credit in Venezuela as Guzmán
saw to it that all payments due under these bond issues were
made promptly. In December of the same year Guzmán
turned his attention to agriculture, organizing a commission
of agriculture and encouraging the cultivation of wheat.[13] He
ordered that seeds in sufficient quantities be bought from
the United States and established special prices for those
engaged in the cultivation of wheat. In the first days of 1871
he established within the ministry of development a general
directorate of statistics, the forerunner of the national census
of Venezuela.

Having stabilized the treasury and assured himself of a
sufficient income, Guzmán Blanco launched an extensive
construction program, the cost of which reached one-and-a-
half-million Venezuelan pesos during six years.[14] A good part
of this sum was used to build streets, squares, markets, aqueducts, and fountains in the cities of Caracas, Valencia,
Puerto Cabello, La Victoria, and others.

From this money there was also constructed the capital
building in Caracas, the central university, a theater, a
museum, and a number of large palaces for the various ministries, the federal court, and the archbishop. The major part
of the money was used to establish better communication
between the leading cities of the republic by the construction
of a number of highways, improvement in the port facilities
of La Guaira and Puerto Cabello, building telegraph services
between the capitals of the states and the federal district,
and finally, beginning construction of a railroad between
Caracas and the port of La Guaira. Guzmán watched as-

[12] *Recopilación de leyes*, V, 94 ff.
[13] *Ibid.*, V, 101.
[14] Hortensio, *Guzmán Blanco y su tiempo*, p. 207.

siduously the development of the work and after the final victory over the Blues, he devoted a major part of his time to inspection trips and inauguration ceremonies for the various highways and public works.

At the beginning of 1871 the president spent several months in Puerto Cabello directing from there both his cabinet in Caracas and his generals in the field. He made several visits to Aragua, Valencia, and Carabobo, consolidating the armies and planning the strategy with generals Salazar, Colina, and Alcántara. Returning to Caracas early in March and confident of ultimate victory, he ordered freed on March 10th all political persons remaining in the prisons and at La Guaira.

Desiring to diminish the bad effects of Archbishop Guevara's expulsion, Guzmán Blanco, during the Holy Week, sent a note and sacred ornaments worth more than ten thousand pesos to Dr. Quintero, Dean of the Archbishopric. On April 19th a *Te Deum* was celebrated and there was a reception in the government house.[15] Thus, a temporary reconciliation with the Church was effected.

On May 11th the president issued a decree on national monies. In this respect, genuine anarchy reigned in the country; foreign monies of gold and silver were being widely used and business disregarded the government conversion table. The new decree referred to monies of gold, silver, and copper and established denominations and values. The standard unit was to be the venezolano and gold monies would have the value of five, ten, and twenty venezolanos. This last was to be called a bolívar. Those of silver were to be called a venezolano, half-venezolano, two-tenths, one-tenth, and five cents and two-and-one-half cents; those of copper to be the cent of eight grams' weight. Specifications on the

---

[15] Aldrey, *Rasgos biográficos*, p. 502.

casts were given and rules decreed for the coining of several types of hard currency.[16]

On May 14th Guzmán Blanco again left the capital to return to Carabobo where General Salazar's conduct was becoming suspicious. General Salazar, once a close supporter of Guzmán Blanco, was evidently developing political ambitions of his own. His issuance of medals, publication of decrees, and unauthorized absence from the front he directed alarmed Guzmán Blanco. Guzmán Blanco's arrival at the front forced Salazar's hand and he made an attempt to bribe the generals under his command and win them over to his side. His attempt failed, and he was sent into exile to return later as a *cause célèbre* in Guzmán Blanco's regime.[17] Having disposed temporarily of Salazar and having reorganized the western front under a new leader, Guzmán Blanco returned to Caracas in the middle of June. The following months Guzmán Blanco spent in Caracas, consolidating his administration, and in Puerto Cabello, planning the final stages of his campaign against the Blues which culminated at the battle of Apure in the decisive defeat of the enemy. While Guzmán Blanco did not participate actively on the battlefield, he exhibited great organizing ability in planning the strategy of the battle of Apure, one of the most interesting episodes in Venezuela's military history. In effect it brought the civil war to an end.[18]

The president reentered Caracas after the victory at Apure on January 27, 1872. Mindful of the forthcoming presidential election, he lent himself willingly to the great outburst of enthusiasm and adulation which marked the end of the civil war. A *Te Deum* by the Church, a gold star in the name of

---

[16] *Recopilación de leyes*, V, 122–24.
[17] Aldrey, *Rasgos biográficos*, pp. 504–21.
[18] *Ibid.*, pp. 521–25.

the Liberal Party, and a banquet by the trade unions of Caracas all demonstrated the personalist element in the devotion to him and strengthened his hold on the people.[19]

The atmosphere was very favorable. The civil war had ended, the local caudillos who had been plaguing Venezuela for decades had been subdued, and the only threat to his undisputed power was offered by Salazar. This threat was eliminated later in the spring when Salazar returned from exile, incited an armed conflict against Guzmán Blanco, was defeated, tried by a military court of twenty-three generals, condemned by the court, and executed.[20]

On June 17, 1872, Guzmán Blanco decreed the convoking of elections. The Constitution of 1864 was to be in force. Popular elections for president of the republic and for deputies were to take place October 1st. Congress was to convene on February 20, 1873, or as soon thereafter as possible, and as of July 1st the military organization of the country was to cease, with only a reserve army as an armed guard. This decree was announced along with a long proclamation which recounted the twenty-five years of fighting against the oligarchy beginning in 1846.[21]

On August 1, 1872, the newspaper *Opinión Nacional* carried an announcement through which Guzmán Blanco made himself known as a candidate for the presidency, despite the fact that he had many times declared "that his mission was fulfilled and that he wished only that the people would elect someone else whom he would gladly support." [22]

Congress convened on February 27, 1873, electing Antonio Leocadio Guzmán president of the senate.[23] On March 1, 1873, Guzmán Blanco appeared before both houses of con-

[19] *Ibid.*, pp. 548–53.
[20] *Ibid.*, pp. 567–75.
[21] *Recopilación de leyes*, V, 141–42.
[22] González Guinán, *Historia contemporánea de Venezuela*, X, 112.
[23] *Ibid.*, X, 168–69.

gress in a resplendent military uniform and gave his presidential message, which was "a torrential exposition of all he had done as leader of the revolution and during the dictatorship, as he himself characterized his action up to that day." [24] He proposed three reforms to the constitution:

1. To change the vote from secret to public.

2. To make all state and national employees responsible to the constitution and general laws of the republic.

3. To reduce the term of president and of all those elected by popular vote to two years.[25]

On April 15, 1873, congress examined the popular votes for president and found 239,691 votes for Guzmán Blanco, 9 for General Pulido, 6 for General Colina, and one each for three other candidates. These figures offer a good example of the technique of unanimity to which many modern dictatorships have notably resorted. Guzmán Blanco, now called Ilustre Americano y Regenerador de Venezuela,[26] was proclaimed president with great fanfare. The next day generals Francisco Linares Alcántara and Joaquín Crespo were elected the first and second designates.[27] General Alcántara soon had a chance to exercise the presidency, since Guzmán Blanco was in those days making frequent trips to the interior to inspect public works and to receive ovations. Not until June 30, 1873, did he again take over the presidency and form his ministry. On March 13, 1874, Guzmán Blanco gave his yearly presidential message and offered to resign his last two years. This offer, however, was refused when his resolution to limit the presidential term was rejected.[28]

[24] Rondón Márquez, Guzmán Blanco, I, 290.
[25] González Guinán, Historia contemporánea de Venezuela, X, 182.
[26] Recopilación de leyes, V, 163.
[27] González Guinán, Historia contemporánea de Venezuela, X, 195.
[28] Discursos del General Guzmán Blanco, pp. 8–9.

In October, 1874, the country's peace was disturbed by the revolt of generals Pulido and Colina in the state of Coro. The former resigned as Inspector General of the Army, saying that he had been accused falsely of receiving land as gifts. The latter, motivated by grudges arising out of local Corian politics, managed to turn the state of Coro against Guzmán Blanco, accusing him of usurping tyrannical power and infringing on the constitutional agreement by sending armed forces into the states to influence elections. The insurrection that followed was actually of advantage to Guzmán Blanco. He came out as victor after a few months of civil war, with Colina surrendering on February 3, 1875. This victory strengthened his position nationally and with individual states.[29]

His prestige at that time was reaching its peak and Guzmán Blanco was the recipient of many honors which were bestowed on him by the national government, the capital, and the several states. Congress had named him Ilustre Americano Regenerador de Venezuela, a title which was ordered used in all public acts. Congress also decreed that the special privileges, the salary, and the honor guard which he had as president should be continued after he left the office. The municipal council of Caracas had a gold medal made in commemoration of the Treaty of Coche. The photograph of Guzmán Blanco was placed by order in all government buildings, in congress, and in the university and numerous streets, squares, and avenues were named after him.

In 1875, two years before the official end of his term, Guzmán Blanco brought public attention to the presidential elections, perhaps in the hope that possible opponents to his prospective candidacy would show their hands and could be removed in plenty of time. In the elections, which took place

[29] Hortensio, *Guzmán Blanco y su tiempo*, pp. 223–25.

in September, 1876, he supported General Alcántara, who was elected and was sworn in office on March 2, 1877.

On handing over the presidency to General Alcántara, Guzmán Blanco delivered an address to the congress in which he claimed credit for many important accomplishments, among which he included the achievement of peace and order in the country, the restoration of electoral liberty, the initiation of educational and social reforms, and the launching of an elaborate program of construction and public works. The congress accepted his address with great enthusiasm and General Alcántara pledged his support and continuance of Guzmán Blanco's policies. The claims made by Guzmán Blanco were justified to some extent, but there were important qualifications and less favorable aspects of his regime which Guzmán Blanco chose to ignore. For a time his injurious use of power, his abnegation of civil rights, and his financial chicanery were veiled by his dominating position and definite material achievements. They were not forgotten, however, and they lay in wait to plague his future career.

CHAPTER VI

New Challenges
and Final Eclipse

After general alcántara took over the presidency, there were still expressions of flattery and adulation for Guzmán Blanco, but it soon became obvious that a new political climate was spreading—for awhile. The voice of relief was heard through the press forecasting a period in which there was to be no imprisonment without trial and no degradation covered by appearances of material progress.[1] Accusations of shady deals entered into circulation, referring to such matters as the nickel negotiations and the railroad construction and, on the whole, it seemed wisest to Guzmán Blanco to take his family and go to Europe for awhile. President Alcántara helped by giving him the position of Venezuela's minister plenipotentiary to Germany, France, Italy, the Vatican, Spain, and Switzerland.

Not for long was Guzmán Blanco to remain outside Venezuela's political life. Though not in power and away in Europe, a continuous controversy was raging over him. The conservatives smarting under repressive measures for seven years after the defeat of the Blue government, the local caudillos shorn of power by Guzmán Blanco and anxious to reestablish their power in their states and regions, and true liberals who were genuinely interested in establishing representative government in Venezuela all voiced their criticism of Guzmán Blanco. On the other hand, his political and military machine countered all complaints with a request for the return of Guzmán Blanco. While General Alcántara was alive

[1] Rondón Márquez, *Guzmán Blanco*, I, 313–14.

his loyalty to Guzmán Blanco prevented any excesses against the latter and kept the opposing factions in check, but with Alcántara's death on November 30, 1878, open conflict broke out. The opponents of Guzmán, boasting a majority in congress, moved for the annulment of the various honors bestowed upon him and demanded the demolition of his statues. The populace took up this cry and on December 12th demolished Guzmán Blanco's statues erected in several parts of the capital.[2]

The destruction of the statues of the man who had been glorified by Venezuela as much as, if not more than, Bolívar provoked a bitter reaction among his followers and seemed also to have sobered other segments of the population. General Cedeño, one of the vice presidents, declared open revolt on the interim government and proclaimed Guzmán Blanco the supreme director of the revolution.[3] In the armed conflict which ensued the revolutionaries, known now as the Reinvindicadores, were successful in mobilizing sizable troops and obtaining the support of leading generals, which won them inevitable victory and the recall of Guzmán Blanco.

Greatly disturbed and mortified by the news of the destruction of his statues, Guzmán Blanco hopefully awaited in Paris the outcome of the revolution and on hearing of the triumph of the Reinvindicadores left for Venezuela, arriving at Caracas on February 25, 1879, where he was received with enthusiasm.[4]

He resumed presidential powers on February 26, 1879, and formed his cabinet. In a previous address on February 21 he had proclaimed his intentions of continuing the interrupted progress of his earlier administration, intimating at the same time that he intended to modify the political system

[2] Hortensio, *Guzmán Blanco y su tiempo*, 294–96.
[3] *Ibid.*, pp. 307–9.
[4] *Ibid.*, p. 323.

by "substitution of the political rights of the Swiss Confederacy for the public rights of the United States of North America, which until now have served us as a model, without the good success achieved by the latter." [5]

On April 27, 1879, Guzmán Blanco called together a congress of plenipotentiaries of the states composed of their respective presidents and representatives. This congress was to direct such institutions as were to remain effective in the country while it returned to constitutional normalcy. It was also to name an interim president of the republic and take up other matters presented to it by the supreme director of the country. [6]

When the congress of plenipotentiaries was convened, Guzmán Blanco asked for the adoption of the following reforms:

1. Reduction of the twenty existing states to seven.

2. A charter of guarantees and individual rights as promised in the 1864 and 1873 constitutions.

3. The introduction of the secret vote.

4. Judicial power to vest in the states with a court of appeal for civil claims.

5. The legislature to be on a four-year basis with the people electing the deputies and the state legislatures naming the senators.

6. A council of state to be created according to the Swiss constitution and to consist of seven senators and fourteen deputies, which council would elect a president every two years from among its members. [7]

[5] *Discursos del General Guzmán Blanco*, p. 114.
[6] *Recopilación de leyes*, VIII, 191.
[7] *Ibid.*, VIII, 192.

The congress did not have the authority to adopt these measures and no further action was taken beyond the election of Guzmán Blanco to the provisional presidency on May 10, 1879.

After the congress adjourned, Guzmán Blanco was granted permission to return to Europe for the purpose of bringing his family to Venezuela.[8] He returned to Caracas on November 24, 1879, where he was, as usual, well received, the enthusiasm reaching so far that all his statues were solemnly restored to their former places of honor.[9]

In December, 1879, Guzmán Blanco once more took over the reins of government, bringing calm to a disturbed country. Apparently quite serious about the suggestions he made to the congress of plenipotentiaries, he called a conference with various military leaders at his ranch, "Guayabita," with the object of enlisting their support for the constitutional reforms he wanted to inaugurate.[10]

On March 13, 1880, election results showed that all twenty states had unanimously voted Guzmán Blanco into the presidency. He was sworn in on March 17th. The main topic on the agenda of the new congress was the constitutional reforms which, after some debate, were finally accepted. The new constitution, however, was not to be ratified until the following year, thus giving Guzmán Blanco two more years of command.[11]

The year 1881 began peacefully. There was the usual New Year's reception at Guzmán Blanco's palatial home, and the president told of various interruptions of the public peace —none of which had lasted more than two weeks—of public works in progress, of schools and colleges that had been

[8] *Ibid.*, VIII, 220.
[9] Hortensio, *Guzmán Blanco y su tiempo*, p. 336.
[10] González Guinán, *Historia contemporánea de Venezuela*, XII, 162.
[11] Rondón Márquez, *Guzmán Blanco*, I, 350.

founded and improved, of adjusted public debts, of consolidated public credit in the interior, and of constitutional reforms to eliminate personalism in the government through the establishment of a federal council.

On April 11th, 1881, Guzmán Blanco ratified Venezuela's sixth constitution, known as the Swiss Constitution because it contained the innovation of a federal council, on the model of Switzerland. It reduced the existing twenty states to nine on the pretext that twenty states were too expensive to administer. The old divisions remained, however, under a governor who was almost a state president, so that there were now twenty old presidents plus nine new ones, creating new rivalries between the state capitals. The object of the change was to have been greater centralization.

A more effective centralizing measure was the decree that provided for the election of the president every two years from the members of the federal council. Although Guzmán Blanco claimed that the reason for this measure was to eliminate personalism, it appears that the real reason may have been the greater probability of unified opinion among the few members of the federal council as compared with the whole congress or the whole nation.

The vote was made direct, public, and obligatory. An electoral census was established to bring order out of confusion. The vote was reserved for those who could read and write and who owned property—in effect, a very rigorous limitation of civil rights. The new constitution was to enter into effect on February 20, 1882.[12]

This new presidential rule of Guzmán Blanco's came to be called the Quinquenio, or five year period, as compared to the earlier Septenio, or seven years, and the later Bienio, or two years. The Quinquenio was outstanding for its activi-

[12] González Guinán, *Historia contemporánea de Venezuela,* XII, 307.

ties in railroad construction, especially on the line from La Guaira to Caracas.[13]

In September, 1881, Guzmán Blanco decreed that in July, 1883, celebrations were to be held for Bolívar's centennial. Although the celebrations turned out to be successful, it was later difficult to say just who was being honored, Bolívar or Guzmán Blanco. Orders were such that Guzmán Blanco's name was mentioned as often as that of the Liberator and the honors given to one were automatically given to the other.[14]

On November 7, 1881, Guzmán Blanco ordered that work be started on the railroad between Puerto Cabello and Valencia. An English engineer, Houston, was in charge of the construction which actually began on November 14th, financed by national funds.[15]

An incident which occurred when the newly elected congress met in March of 1882, demonstrated how little importance Guzmán Blanco and his ministers attached to the constitutional reforms they had introduced. After Guzmán Blanco delivered his presidential message before congress on March 6, 1882, he was asked by Secretary of Interior Amengual if he would accept the presidency for the following two years and not leave Venezuela at the mercy of new chaos and disorder.[16] The question was entirely out of order since the new constitution had clearly provided that congress was to elect the president from the members of the federal council, among whom Guzmán Blanco did not figure. The latter did not answer Secretary Amengual, but neither did he call his attention to the new decree of the constitution. On March 11th his name was included among the members

[13] Ibid., XII, 316.
[14] Briceño, Los ilustres, p. 212.
[15] González Guinán, Historia contemporánea de Venezuela, XII, 363.
[16] Ibid., XII, 363.

elected to the federal council, thus vitiating the new constitution at its very beginning. On March 13th Guzmán Blanco was unanimously elected to the Venezuelan presidency for the period from 1882 to 1884 and was sworn in on March 17, 1882.[17]

When Congress went into recess on May 27, 1882, it had passed the following legislation:

1. The establishment of a thirty percent additional tax on merchandise from the Antilles, a measure through which Guzmán Blanco revenged himself on the commerce of those islands, which he considered hotbeds of political discontent against him.

2. The approval of a treaty between Venezuela and Colombia, transferring the old boundary disputes to the arbitration of the king of Spain.

3. The permission to erect a statue to Antonio Leocadio Guzmán, with a series of exaggerated inscriptions.

4. The granting of extraordinary authority to the president.

5. The approval of numerous contracts for the exploitation of national resources and building of railroads.[18]

Venezuelan economic conditions in 1883 were still far from satisfactory, although public debt bonds were being quoted at a good price and industry was being fostered with private capital as a sign of confidence in the country's stability. There was a locust plague which ruined the fruit crop and continued its ravages from Maracay to Caracas. The price of coffee and other fruits for export continued to decline. There was, however, growing enthusiasm for the coming centennial celebrations of Bolívar. Furthermore, in June, 1883, together with the unpleasant locust plague there ar-

---

[17] *Ibid.*, XII, 414.
[18] *Ibid.*, XII, 439–40.

Antonio Leocadio Guzmán

rived at the outskirts of Caracas the first locomotive train from La Guaira.[19]

Great was the flattery and numerous were the signs of enthusiasm and adoration offered to Guzmán Blanco on his trip to Carabobo and Aragua at the end of the Quinquenio. Equally great was the vanity of the president, as seen in his speech at a banquet at Villa de Cura:

For my successor there are only two choices: the way of Guz-mán Blanco who, finding nothing, had to create everything . . . ; or the way of Alcántara who, having everything, lost everything through his personal plans and rapacious ambitions and his dis-loyal behavior. There will be two horizons open to the elected: one which will blazon the dishonor and shame of Alcántara and another of glory through the gratitude and love of the people, which is that of Guzmán Blanco.[20]

On April 27, 1884, General Joaquín Crespo became presi-dent of Venezuela.[21] There were several other candidates but Guzmán Blanco's preference for Crespo decided the elec-tion. In June, 1884, Guzmán Blanco, satisfied with the way things were going, left for Europe as envoy extraordinary and minister plenipotentiary to Great Britain, Belgium, Spain, Italy, and the Vatican.[22]

While his son was in Europe, Antonio Leocadio Guzmán died on November 13, 1884, in Caracas, and was buried amidst extensive manifestations of honor.

The administration of Crespo did not begin under favor-able auspices. As in previous periods when Guzmán gave up the presidency, hidden passions surged to the surface and denunciations and recriminations against him became the order of the day. This contributed to the creation of internal

[19] *Ibid.*, XII, 511.
[20] *Ibid.*, XII, 67.
[21] *Ibid.*, XIII, 100.
[22] *Ibid.*, XIII, 133.

unrest in the country. Venezuela's economic situation also deteriorated greatly.

The effects of the locust plague which reduced the production of foodstuffs, the critical condition of the coffee industry because of the deterioration of the product and poor harvests, the complete decline of the sugar cane industry, and the general commercial crisis which these agricultural conditions produced affected the economy of the entire country.[23]

Exploiting these circumstances, a number of Guzmán's friends grouped around *La Opinión Nacional* and played heavily on the theme that Guzmán Blanco would be the only man to bring order into the political and economic chaos of Venezuela.

Guzmán Blanco wrote from London in May, 1885, saying:

I will not accept the presidency because it would soil the glory of the Liberal Party as well as sacrifice my reputation because of the many years that I have headed the country. Any good liberal is capable of filling the presidency during the next constitutional period.[24]

He was elected to congress and the federal council the following year by a unanimity that seemed both strange and imposing. He appeared as senator-elect from every state, along with the other two constitutionally designated ones, as no state wanted to cede the honor of electing Guzmán Blanco. The congress elected him to the presidency by a unanimous vote on March 27, 1886.[25]

Guzmán Blanco arrived at Caracas on August 28, 1886, amidst apparently genuine, enthusiastic demonstrations of welcome. He would have come sooner but he had to delay

[23] *Ibid.*, XIII, 278.
[24] *Ibid.*, XIII, 253.
[25] *Ibid.*, XIII, 309.

his trip until he had seen his daughter, Carlota, safely married off to the French duke of Morny.[26]

On September 15, 1886, Guzmán Blanco took the oath of office, at which time Crespo presented him with a medal, "Sol de Perú," which had belonged to the Liberator. Thanking Crespo for this honor, Guzmán Blanco immediately announced that he would deposit the medal in the national museum. That same day, too, Guzmán Blanco formed his ministry, which included mainly adherents of General Crespo and, consequently, of Guzmán Blanco.

With the return of Guzmán Blanco to power, stability and economic recovery appeared to return to the country. The economic situation actually began to improve. The titles of the public debt began to rise in price, and Guzmán Blanco rejected a loan from Trujillo when it could not be obtained in the name of the government.

Before long, Guzmán Blanco returned to his sumptuous estate at Antimano, a kind of Versailles à la Guzmán Blanco where he received his ministers every day, forcing them to take long carriage rides out there to see him. From time to time he would come to Caracas to inspect public works and receive public adulation.[27]

One of the first things the president did was to revise numerous contracts made during Crespo's administration. He also ordered the reimbursement of funds taken for other uses from the income budget of public instruction. To avoid making any reflection on Crespo's administrative acts, Guzmán Blanco ordered that the presidential salary be paid to Crespo throughout his lifetime.[28]

Toward the end of the year Guzmán Blanco was in Caracas to assist at the inauguration of a railway line between

[26] Rondón Márquez, *Guzmán Blanco*, I, 403.
[27] Briceño, *Los ilustres*, pp. 232–33.
[28] González Guinán, *Historia contemporánea de Venezuela*, XIII, 374.

Caracas and Petare and at the inauguration of a mint which had been installed to coin money in the country with advance payments from European houses based on contracts made by Guzmán Blanco while still in Paris.[29]

During the first months of his administration the president also took time to smooth out the internal difficulties of the various states. As a result of his intervention strife and political assassinations diminished.

Before the year was up, the unconditionals, as Guzmán Blanco's faithful partisans were called, made motions to reform the constitution and Guzmán Blanco refused to consider another term immediately after the present one.[30]

The idea, nevertheless, did seem to please Guzmán Blanco, for at the beginning of 1887 he decided to give free run to the press to sound out public opinion. In short time he found out that there was substantial opposition to him in the country. Certain newspapers were even spreading the idea of organizing a new party, the Nationalist Party, a plan which did not meet with Guzmán Blanco's approval. As a consequence, he had some papers suppressed and their editors sent to jail.[31]

After the newsmen had been imprisoned, opposition became even stronger. Various plots were made against the president's life, the first planned to take place at Antimano, another at the Guzmán Blanco Theater, a third in the baths of a Señor Soucy at El Calvario, and the final attempt at the funeral of Señora Romana Blanco, the president's aunt. The plans did not succeed for various reasons, but as a result there were many imprisonments, the states were alerted, opposition newspapers were suspended, and manifestations were forbidden. Arms supplies were placed in strategic places, espe-

[29] *Ibid.*, XIII, 378.
[30] *Ibid.*, XIII, 402–5.
[31] *Ibid.*, XIII, 489.

cially at Valencia, and military bodies were reorganized and prepared for emergencies.[32]

Congress closed its sessions on May 27, 1887, after having approved various laws and many contracts made by Guzmán Blanco in Europe. After the representatives returned to their respective states, there began the electoral agitations for regional presidents. Nothing had as yet been done about national elections, everyone waiting for Guzmán Blanco to declare himself. There was a division between adherents of Guzmán Blanco and of General Crespo, and in order to eliminate this conflict Guzmán Blanco left on June 21, 1887, to meet Crespo in Maracay. Their meeting, however, was not successful, for the two men broke off all relations.

Guzmán Blanco informed his friends that he had no intention of being reelected but that he did not want Crespo to succeed him. In July, 1887, Crespo and his family went to Europe, the general feeling quite confident that he would obtain the presidency at the next election. He had not counted, however, on Guzmán Blanco, who arranged matters so that two other candidates, González Guinán and Rojas Paúl, came to be the final contestants for the presidency.[33]

Among the last acts of Guzmán Blanco's administration were the inauguration of the famous bridge of Guanábana in Caracas; the celebration of various contracts, among which was one with his son-in-law, the duke of Morny, to pipe the aqueduct from Maracoa; another with the painter, Erwin Cheme, to paint a picture of the Congress of Angostura; one with the North American Company to construct new piers and storage houses in Puerto Cabello for two million bolivars; and one with Manuel Hernaiz to build a sugar factory like the ones in Cuba.[34] He wanted to terminate his adminis-

[32] *Ibid.*, XIII, 513–14.
[33] *Ibid.*, XIII, 576–77.
[34] *Ibid.*, XIII, 580–83.

tration with a number of decrees for public works and orders for the continuation of others, all of which were in charge of special development councils to which he delivered around a million-and-a-half bolivars for completion. Finally, he parcelled out among his friends in public service one 'million bolivars, an act which was greatly criticized since it was motivated by a desire to leave a good impression among his followers.[35] To the national museum he sent numerous objects which had belonged to the Liberator and other founders of Venezuela, among which was the "Sol de Perú." He reserved the right of recovery of this object if it were removed from the museum.[36]

Handing over the presidency to General Hermógenes López until a new president should be elected, Guzmán Blanco left Venezuela, for what was to be the last time, to return to Europe. His speech on the occasion of his departure struck his listeners as being less ostentatious than ever before. Perhaps he felt that his reign was really at its end at last.[37]

When election time drew near Guzmán Blanco, from Europe, supported Dr. Rojas Paúl, a fact which leads one to believe that the former president was more interested in maintaining his influence from outside than he was in Venezuela's internal order and stability.

The congress, convening on June 29, 1888, elected the federal council which met on July 2, and named Rojas Paúl president of Venezuela for the Bienio of 1888 to 1890.[38]

In Europe, Guzmán Blanco received the news of Rojas Paúl's election with satisfaction, inasmuch as Paúl was one of his partisans from whom he expected full cooperation whenever necessary. It had cost Guzmán Blanco some effort to elevate Paúl to the presidency, and it is, therefore, under-

[35] *Ibid.*, XIII, 587.
[36] *Ibid.*, XIII, 589.
[37] Rondón Márquez, *Guzmán Blanco*, I, 421–24.
[38] González Guinán, *Historia contemporánea de Venezuela*, XIV, 113.

standable that he took pride in his achievement. Guzmán
Blanco's joy and hope, however, were shortlived. Dr. Rojas
Paúl confirmed Guzmán as Venezuela's plenipotentiary minister before several nations of Europe and granted him the
right to make contracts on behalf of his government,[39] but
hostile symptoms against him at home began to appear when
congress discussed a contract that he had made with José
Antonio Salas and Felipe Tejera to construct a network of
sewers in Caracas for the sum of nine million bolivars. After
a heated discussion, during which some questions were
raised regarding the integrity of Guzmán Blanco's administration, the contracts remained unapproved.[40]

Came the year 1889 and Guzmán Blanco was beginning to
be impatient. With every boat that arrived from Europe he
sent projects for new contracts—railroads, a Franco-Egyptian
Bank, a factory of "maicena," unification of the debt, immigration, etc. With great diplomacy Rojas Paúl always
delayed action by not submitting the various contracts to
congress or by sending them to those who he knew were least
interested in supporting them.[41]

This was supplemented by the fact that after President
Rojas Paúl had sent an extensive letter to Guzmán Blanco,
in which he told him all the details about the defeat of
General Crespo, his letters to Guzmán Blanco became little
more than short notes. He excused himself on the ground that
too much work and worry made him incapable of carrying
on an extensive correspondence. Guzmán refused to accept
this explanation and a rupture between the two men was
imminent.

On the occasion of Guzmán Blanco's sixtieth birthday,
February 28, 1889, his friends received permission from gov-

[39] *Ibid.*, XIV, 144.
[40] *Ibid.*, XIV, 150–56.
[41] Rondón Márquez, *Guzmán Blanco*, II, 24–5.

ernment authorities in Venezuela to organize public festivals. As a final flare-up of earlier adoration, Guzmán Blanco's monuments were illuminated and even the president and the cabinet placed a wreath of flowers at the monument in the capital. There were also those inevitable groups of students, however, who added noise and color through catcalls and whistling. Opposition papers did not fail to heap ridicule on the celebrations. It was fairly obvious that there was little sentiment except protocol underlying the festivities. They turned out to be the last ones given to the Regenerator in public.[42]

There could be no further doubt that Guzmán Blanco's influence in Venezuela was at an end. President Rojas Paúl in his message to congress in February, 1889, did not mention Guzmán Blanco's contracts which had been sent from Europe, a fact of which Guzmán was well aware.[43]

This attitude on the part of the government of Rojas Paúl reached its climax when an advantageous agreement, assuring Venezuela of a reduction in interest paid on its foreign loans, was negotiated by Guzmán Blanco in London but was killed by the indifference and hostility of President Paúl and his cabinet.[44]

Subsequently, the anniversary (April 27th) of the capture in 1870 of Caracas by Guzmán Blanco, which had been celebrated for many years with great demonstrations in honor of Guzmán Blanco, also ended tragically for him. Hostile manifestations were staged throughout the city and groups of students attacked Guzmán Blanco's monuments and ran through the streets of Caracas shouting, "Down with tyranny. Death to Guzmán Blanco. Long live Rojas Paúl!"[45] Similar anti-Guzmán Blanco outbursts occurred also in La Guaira.

[42] Ibid., II, 29–30.
[43] González Guinán, Historia contemporánea de Venezuela, XIV, 299.
[44] Ibid., XIV, 307–12.
[45] Ibid., XIV, 330–31.

The government took little action to stop them and the unconditional Guzmanists in the cabinet resigned.[46]

Guzmán Blanco, who was informed in Paris of these demonstrations, thought it best to hand in his resignation to the minister of the exterior. Rojas Paúl, however, did not consider the resignation and merely set it aside. Thus, Guzmán Blanco stayed on in France doing what he liked best. He was Venezuela's representative at the centennial celebration of the French Revolution and arranged for the presentation of Venezuela's gift to the president of France, a bust of Bolívar.[47]

When presidential elections began drawing near in Venezuela, anti-Guzmán Blanco reaction became stronger and more open. On October 26, 1889, a statue of Guzmán Blanco in Caracas was pulled down by a group of university students. Other statues of Guzmán Blanco suffered the same fate that night, and his house in Camoruco was sacked.[48] Thus began the process of demolition of all the statues and monuments that Venezuela had erected to its Regenerator, supreme dictator, and president for many years. The government did little to stop these excesses against Guzmán Blanco, for by that time Guzmán Blanco and Rojas Paúl had come to the end of their friendship. The latter now felt himself free of all his ties to Guzmán Blanco, and the cabinet slowly but steadily received the appointments of anti-Guzmán Blanco men. When, in 1890, Rojas Paúl stepped out of the presidency, not only was Guzmán Blanco's hegemony in Venezuela ended but the once powerful Liberal Party was helplessly and completely split up.

The inertia of age and the love of luxury were responsible for Guzmán Blanco's final downfall. When President Paúl

[46] Ibid., XIV, 341.
[47] Rondón Márquez, Guzmán Blanco, II, 48–9.
[48] González Guinán, Historia contemporánea de Venezuela, XIV, 459–60.

began to disregard his messages and contracts, Guzmán Blanco still had many supporters in the cabinet and among the military. Had he returned to Venezuela, the course of his personal history might have been different. The hold of Gómez on Venezuela in the twentieth century argues favorably for this assumption. Guzmán Blanco, however, indulging in his splendor in Paris, apparently did not have the real will to return and fight for his domain, and his failure to take vigorous action discouraged his faithful supporters and spelled the eclipse of his regime and of his party.

He spent the following ten years of his life in Paris engaging in long distance polemics but actually enjoying the grand life that his wealth and personal charm, as well as European credulity, assured him. He died in Paris on July 30, 1899. By that time, Venezuelan passions were calmed with regard to him, and his death provoked real sorrow in the country, best exemplified by an editorial in the Caracas *Cojo Ilustrado* on August 15, 1899, which read:

On the 30th day of the last month General Antonio Guzmán Blanco died in Paris. He was 71 years old. . . . Now is not the time either to praise or to condemn the work of Guzmán Blanco as a politician, statesman, or reformer. His political labor represented a variety of triumphs and defeats which still move the political organization of the country.

Triumphs and defeats—along the broken road of a caudillo, who so often ended his days in exile when he did not suffer a more violent fate.

CHAPTER VII

Aspects of a Caudillo Regime:
Ideological Irresponsibility

Now that the facts of Guzmán Blanco's political career have been presented, it remains to analyze some of the aspects that went into that career—aspects that are, for the most part, intrinsic to the caudillo type of regime in Latin America. The basic considerations are what may be called ideological irresponsibility, the unqualified use of force, financial chicanery, and personalism.

Although such a versatile and picturesque personality as Antonio Guzmán Blanco possesses a larger number of traits, this study is confined to those four general characteristics which were projected decisively into the system of his government, were responsible for the spirit and form of his rule, and are found in the basic structure of any caudillo phenomenon.

Because his personal will was the essence of the rule of Guzmán Blanco, it was inevitable that his policies were not directed by adherence to any conviction or any set of principles. The European dictators, whether they be fascists or communists, emphasize strongly a set of ideals as the guiding motives of their regime. They may indeed diverge from these ideals, but at least they seek, for the most part, to maintain some kind of coherent ideology. Although Guzmán Blanco professed adherence to the liberal cause on many occasions, the entire history of his government indicates a constant shifting of objectives, a continuous change in legislation, a frequent reversal of program ideas, and a total lack of responsibility toward policies, principles, and alliances.[1]

An element of opportunism is found in all political behavior. It is a feature that is apt, in some degree, to accompany the process of any decision making; it is singled out and
attributed, therefore, only when, as in the case of Guzmán
Blanco, it is present in a high degree. In such a case this
feature is closely related to the element of ideological responsibility.

The opportunism of Guzmán Blanco was clearly evident
throughout his career. A politician without principles and
a master of political scheming, Guzmán Blanco utilized to
the utmost the opportunist approach.

As a young man in Caracas, the son of an aristocratic
family whose father was prominent in politics, he was often
called upon to deliver public addresses. Considering the
conflict which existed then in Venezuela between the Catholic Church and the more liberal elements, young Antonio
Guzmán made certain not to become identified with either
group. On invitation, he delivered a speech at a Catholic
ceremony before the Society of Maria, but balanced it immediately with a funeral oration before a Masonic lodge.

Young Antonio Guzmán continued his pleasant and un-
eventful career until his father was exiled from Venezuela by
the conservatives and the son found it expedient to go with
him. In joining his father in exile, he also espoused the Liberal Party and the federation movement. His actions show,
however, that he was not motivated by the acceptance of
the ideals of that party but by the realization that as a son
of Antonio Leocadio Guzmán he would be rejected by the

---

[1] In this respect Guzmán followed the strategy advocated by Machiavelli,
whose advice was: "A wise lord cannot, nor ought he to, keep faith when
such observance may be turned against him, and when the reasons that
caused him to pledge it exist no longer . . . nor will there ever be wanting
to a prince legitimate reasons to excuse his non-observance" (Nicolo Machiavelli, *The Prince,* edited and translated by W. K. Marriott).

conservatives and that, therefore, his future lay with the Liberal Party and the movement for federation.

As the next logical step, he joined up with General Juan Falcón, who headed the federation forces in the revolution which lasted four years and is known as the Federal War. Little concerned by the issues of the war, young Antonio, realizing that military command and economic wealth were the vehicles to power, embarked upon attaining these two aims.

In the federation forces there were two strong personalities, General Juan Falcón, an impractical and vainglorious idealist, and General Ezequiel Zamora, an uncouth and uneducated caudillo, but a man of outstanding bravery and military ability. Young Antonio Guzmán proceeded to fan the conflict between these two people and at the same time to ingratiate himself with both so that he was soon looked upon as the mediator between them. He began the publication of the newspaper called the *Eco del Ejército* in which he played up to the vanity of Falcón, who made him secretary general of the federation. Simultaneously, by professing great admiration for the military skill of Zamora, he also gained the confidence of the latter. Having established himself in the confidence of both, he accomplished his first objective—that of a military career. He was permitted to participate, although at a safe distance, in several battles, primarily that of Sabana de la Cruz, and was soon promoted to colonel. Ezequiel Zamora was killed at San Carlos. The Falcón forces suffered a defeat at Coplé and Falcón found it necessary to seek asylum with his staff in Colombia, but Guzmán Blanco, holding on now unconditionally to Falcón, continued to advance. When a new expedition was formed and the war resumed on the territory of Venezuela, young Antonio was promoted to the rank of general and soon found himself in charge of the very strategic central front, superseding a number of important generals. His political ability came to the fore. Being the youngest in age and in seniority of rank, he was looked upon with suspicion by the other chiefs. Instead of putting pressure upon them to accept his supreme command, he embarked on a campaign of dividing the generals and caudillos of the center. He maneuvered them around so that they finally came to depend upon him for advice, conciliation, and coordination. In a short time he was undisputed master of the center and, for all practical purposes, the leader of the federation forces.

Having acquired the first objective on his road to power, namely, military prominence, he now turned to his second goal, economic wealth. A Venezuela immersed in a bloody conflict was hardly a propitious field for economic advancement, and Guzmán Blanco soon lost interest in the war and in military conquests and began to look for means of achieving peace. In the Páez government he found a counterpart to himself in the person of Pedro José Rojas, secretary general of Páez. Without consulting or obtaining the authorization of Falcón, Guzmán Blanco, on his own account, began what amounted to secret approaches to the enemy. He established contact with Rojas and a number of meetings followed between the two, culminating in the Treaty of Coche. While peace in Venezuela may have been one of the motives of the negotiations which led to the Treaty of Coche, there is incontrovertible proof that a decisive role in Guzmán Blanco's anxiety to arrange a peace treaty was played by an existing loan contracted from England through the Baring Brothers and by the possibility of a larger loan from England on which negotiations had already begun with the Páez government. This assumption is borne out by the facts that after Guzmán Blanco, with the aid of Falcón's brother-in-law, General Jacinto Pachano, had succeeded in having Falcón accept the treaty against his own wishes and that after the inauguration of the Falcón government in Caracas, Antonio Guzmán Blanco left immediately for England to negotiate the loan. By his own admission, it was the beginning of his fortune and assured him of the second step in his career—that of economic wealth.

While Falcón was in power in the years from 1863 to 1867, Guzmán Blanco devoted his time to two personal objectives. First was the economic one. He commuted between Venezuela, London, and Paris negotiating loans and contracts and making certain that large commissions and continuous revenues would accrue to him. He was so successful in his efforts that early in 1879 he was able to say: "Mi fortuna es poco común en America (My fortune is not common in America)." [2]

His second preoccupation was to build his political future. Outwardly he professed great admiration for President Falcón; actually, he did everything to show up the weakness of Falcón, exploiting his dislike of Caracas and his frequent absences from the capital. Guzmán Blanco, in spite of his many trips to Europe, made certain that he was in Caracas when Falcón went away and that he, as the first designate or vice president, assumed the presidency during Falcón's absence. In building up his political future he showed great consideration for all parties and leaders. He successfully concealed the autocratic tendencies which appeared later when he was the undisputed master of Venezuela. He conciliated the warring caudillos, which Falcón could not do. He presented to congress constructive measures which were extremely important at this stage of Venezuela's political stabilization and administrative reorganization. When the contrast of his competence with Falcón's lack of it became very striking and his personal enemies called Falcón's attention to Guzmán Blanco's ambitious plans, he successfully

[2] *La reivindicación,* p. 41.

allayed Falcón's suspicions for awhile by playing on his vanity and by having congress confer on him the title of Grand Marshal of the Republic.

When he realized that Falcón had neither the support nor the respect of the country, he left for Europe, knowing that without his assistance Falcón's government would not survive. A series of uprisings took place in Venezuela. Falcón was eliminated and General Bruzual carried on the government for a short time. He was followed by the old General Monagas and finally by the latter's nephew, General Ruperto Monagas. Guzmán Blanco, safely away in Paris with no need to participate either in the defense of Falcón or in the subsequent conflict, watched the developments.

Having assured himself that Falcón was definitely eliminated and that it would be unnecessary for him to defend the Grand Marshal, Guzmán Blanco returned to Venezuela to don Falcón's mantle. He sought to become the leader of the liberals and at first encountered considerable opposition from them because they had not forgotten his financial manipulations and his abandonment of Falcón. The Liberal Party, however, divided between collaborationists and oppositionists, had no personality strong enough to challenge Guzmán Blanco's claim to the leadership. He intentionally called attention to his liberal and oppositionist tendencies and because of his prominence soon became the target of attacks by the government and the populace of Caracas. This culminated in the episode of August 14, 1869, when, during a reception to which the most prominent families of Caracas and of the diplomatic corps were invited, his home was attacked and he and his guests had to defend themselves. Whatever the origin of the attack, it accomplished Guzmán Blanco's purpose. It evoked great sympathy for him among the impartial citizens of Caracas and brought out the loyalty of a number of caudillos throughout the country who had dealings with him during the Federal War and the Falcón regime, thus forcing the Liberal party to accept him as the leader.

After a series of escapes which included hiding out in the Embassy of the United States of America, Guzmán Blanco fled from Caracas to La Guaira and from there by boat to Curaçao, but the war against the government was already being carried on in his behalf. General Pulido in Barrinas, General Colina in Coro, Crespo in El Guarico, Salazar in Carabobo, Mendoza in El Tuy—all of them had taken up arms. Guzmán Blanco took advantage of these uprisings to unify and to give cohesion to his separate efforts. At the same time he engaged in a voluminous correspondence with the partisans of the government he was fighting and with other influential elements in the country, especially the merchants of Caracas and La Guaira. He assured them in his letters that he had no vindictive purposes and that he was interested only in establishing peace and order in the country.

The effect of this correspondence was of great importance, as Guzmán Blanco was remembered for the years of peace and stability which Venezuela enjoyed when he was substituting for Falcón. The military exploits of the caudillos and the diplomatic maneuvers of Guzmán Blanco were successful. Although peace did not come until 1872, a large part of the country was conquered by his army, and on April 27, 1870, he entered Caracas, no longer the glorified underling of Falcón but, in his own right, the absolute ruler of Venezuela. In eleven years, from the time that he joined Falcón in the Federal War in 1859, he accomplished the two great objectives of his life—economic fortune and undisputed political power in Venezuela.

Knowing full well that his strength depended on the loyalty of the several generals of his armies and intent on eliminating any attempt at insurrection on their part, he seized upon the uprising of General Salazar as an act of national treason to strike terror in the hearts of other generals who might have contemplated similar action. He played up the revolt of Salazar, one of his former intimate friends and supporters, with such great skill that the generals themselves demanded the harshest punishment for Salazar and twenty-three of them formed a special court to condemn him and order his execution. While Guzmán Blanco's expectation that the Salazar incident would serve as a deterrent factor was not fully realized (time and again some caudillo took up arms against him), such actions were isolated and represented no real threat either to his prestige or to his government. Guzmán Blanco's action in the case of Salazar was not the only one where he turned against a friend and supporter. Having established himself in power, he began to plan the elimination or neutralization of the military leaders who had brought him to power. He was determined to allow no competition on the national scale and he embarked on a campaign of sowing distrust and dissension. Venezuela, since the Federal War, had been a collection of armed camps headed by several national, and many secondary, chieftains. By favoring now the secondary caudillos and by using either adverse propaganda or repressive measures against the more nationally known caudillos, Guzmán Blanco was able to control them and assure himself of an undisputed hold over the country.

In his dealings with another very important factor in the life of Venezuela, the Catholic Church, Guzmán Blanco exhibited the same shrewd opportunism that characterized his entire government, managing to maneuver between the Catholic society and the Masonic lodge.

The most genuine statement of Guzmán Blanco with respect to his beliefs is perhaps contained in a fragment from his speech at the inauguration of a Masonic temple in Caracas:

There was a time in which religious fanaticism oppressed the conscience of the people; then the Masonic temples were opened so that all the nations could freely adore, without concern for any external cult, the Great Creator who did not populate the world with Christians and Mohammedans, with Jews and Protestants, and with members of the Egyptian and of the Asiatic religions so that they should kill each other, but who populated it instead with equal creatures who adore Him with one single prayer as the celestial spheres adore Him with their immortal and harmonious hymn.[3]

In this passage Guzmán Blanco expressed his approval of the Masonic temples as opposed to the individual churches of various religions. According to him, the separate churches provoked discord and hatred among their members while the Masonic temples united them all in the service and love of one God.

His first conflict with the Church occurred in 1867 when the archdeacon of the Cathedral of Caracas, Father Antonio José Sucre, attempted to refuse the use of one of its cemeteries for the burial of a Mason. Guzmán Blanco sought the intervention of Archbishop Guevara, with whom he was then on good terms, and Father Sucre, who henceforth remained a bitter enemy of Guzmán Blanco's, was sent to Europe. The second incident, inspired by the same Father Sucre, occurred during the Blue Revolution when it became evident that Catholic priests openly supported the Blue forces against Guzmán Blanco and his liberals. The next step in the conflict came about when Archbishop Guevara of Venezuela refused the request of the minister of the interior, made on September 26, 1870, that a *Te Deum* be celebrated to commemorate a victory of the Guzmán forces. Archbishop Gue-

[3] *Discursos del General Guzmán Blanco*, p. 75.

vara refused to arrange this celebration of a fratricidal war until such time as a general amnesty was declared in Venezuela. As a result of this refusal, the archbishop was expelled from Venezuela[4] and although Guzmán Blanco disclaimed this incident, saying that it would not have happened had he been in Caracas at that time, he did nothing to appease the archbishop.

Guzmán Blanco realized that the power of the Church depended in large measure on its great economic strength, on its control of christenings, marriages, and funerals, and on the great holdings of its many convents and monasteries. He proceeded ruthlessly to demolish the strength of the Church. He ordered closed and expropriated the properties of a number of convents and seminaries[5] and introduced a law which permitted civil marriages and required all parishioners to register all christenings, marriages, and burials performed by them with the civil authorities.[6] At the very beginning of his own regime in 1870, he struck the hardest blow at the economic position of the Church. Since the Church owned large properties which it had leased or sold, he ordered that the annual rental on such properties could be paid to the Church not in effective cash, but in public debt bonds. This deprived the Church immediately of a large cash income. Two years later he prohibited the Church from holding large tracts of lands which were not cultivated, claiming that it remained in "dead hands."[7] Thirdly, he discontinued the payment of national contributions to the Church, stating that any contribution should be made on a voluntary basis.[8] During this time, Archbishop Guevara continued in his exile on the island of St. Thomas and refused

[4] González Guinán, *Historia contemporánea de Venezuela*, IX, 437.
[5] *Recopilación de leyes*, V, 272.
[6] *Ibid.*, V, 177.
[7] *Ibid.*, V, 223.
[8] *Ibid.*, V, 252, 254.

either to accept Guzmán Blanco's terms or to resign his post. Guzmán Blanco struck further against the Church by having congress pass a law establishing an independent Catholic Church in Venezuela and by making the post of the archbishop of Venezuela subject to election by congress.[9] The Church, alarmed by Guzmán Blanco's steps, agreed to the resignation of Archbishop Guevara and to the appointment of Archbishop Ponte,[10] who was acceptable to Guzmán Blanco; but most of the damage was already done. Guzmán magnanimously rescinded the congressional declaration of an independent church of Venezuela, but his economic legislation remained in effect.

His relation to the Church in later years was characterized by the same opportunism. In a message to congress in 1873 he said:

It was because of my sincere love and faith in God that I accepted the responsibilities of the dictatorship. Only led by the will of Providence could I believe myself capable of assuming the immensity of the duties which are imposed upon me by the past, the present, and the future of my country.[11]

Here he declared himself to be a good Catholic, whose life and actions were guided by the will of destiny.

But again on April 27, 1876, he said:

The Roman oligarchy is incompatible with our republican practices; the pontificate cannot exist at the same time as the republic. The former, with all the superiority and magnitude of the ancient *Caesara*, to whom it owes its primitive power, aspires, without considering the civilization and the necessities of our present times, to perpetuate its empire, using as a lever the responsiveness of the human spirit. On the other hand, the republic, which is the expression of the popular world, sanctions liberty of thought

---

[9] *Actos legislativos.*
[10] González Guinán, *Historia contemporánea de Venezuela*, XI, 86.
[11] *Discursos del General Guzmán Blanco*, p. 18.

and liberty of sentiment as its most honorable political conquest. It is the struggle of intolerant absolutism with new ideas and modern right.[12]

Here he reverted to his struggle with the Catholic Church. He emphasized that it was impossible for a democratic republic with modern ideas to cooperate with a pontificate which drew its dogmas and policies from the ancient practices of the Roman oligarchy. The Church was the representative of intolerance and demanded absolute obedience, while the modern republic represented liberty of thought and liberty of expression.

But again on April 27, 1881, he found it expedient to return to the fold with the following words:

The Church has been for ten centuries the torch of civilization. The world owes to it the treasure of its present science, the morality which it has founded, and the enlightenment of the peoples, so that there are no more peoples sunk in darkness in any part of the world—and all this is due to the Church.[13]

The same shifting of position which characterized Guzmán Blanco's actions prior to arrival at supreme power in Venezuela was evident in his actions throughout the eighteen years, 1870 to 1888, when his word was the law in Venezuela. The civil war ended in 1872. The unruly caudillos were liquidated or subdued and the Church was forced to come to terms. There remained his main preoccupation—that of maintaining and perpetuating himself in power in a "constitutional" way. During the war years he was the chief of the revolution and the supreme dictator of the republic, but after the capture of Caracas in April of 1870, a congress of plenipotentiaries was called to meet in Caracas to elect a provisional president.

[12] *Ibid.*, 77 ff.
[13] *Ibid.*, p. 155.

In a message to the congress on June 15, 1870, disclaiming any desire for the office of provisional president, he said:

I can say that my mission has been fulfilled. It consisted of uniting and directing the popular efforts to bring about the defeat of the usurpatory power of the oligarchy. After the presidential victory, I could be suspected of an ambition if I did not anticipate it by declaring that you should elect as president a citizen whose past record and services would dispel any fear of his becoming tempted by power, willingly or unwillingly. By the very fact that I have been the chief of the revolution and because it has fallen to my lot to gain the victory, you must consider me as the most incompetent to deserve the election.[14]

In this statement Guzmán pointed out all the dangers that his continuance in office would mean for the country. He warned that his designation would be unwise because it would expose him to temptation by power, and he stressed his conclusion that anyone who had brought victory and peace to the country and might, therefore, have intentions of using these achievements as a pretext to power, was the most incompetent person for office.

This ringing declaration was made to a congress consisting of fifteen delegates who had been designated by the presidents of the particular states and whose authority came as a result of the armed conflict and, therefore, of the favor of the chief of the revolution. His noble declaration was as nobly rejected by the fifteen delegates and he was persuaded to accept the election to the provisional presidency, not, however, without taking the opportunity to declare on July 22, 1870:

My opinion was, as you know, that you should have preferred some other Venezuelan; but in the midst of the crisis in which we find ourselves, a refusal on my part to accept a post of more work,

[14] *Ibid.*

more danger, and greater responsibilities would expose me to interpretations which the Fatherland, the liberal cause, and my own honor advise me to avoid.[15]

While he maintained here that some other man should have been chosen for office, he would not refuse the post given to him because he would not like an unfavorable interpretation placed on such a refusal.

The following two years Guzmán Blanco enjoyed full power as provisional president, or, as he himself called it, supreme dictator of Venezuela. When the civil war came to an end in May of 1872, Guzmán Blanco returned to Caracas on May 30th in great triumph, being welcomed by a *Te Deum* in the cathedral, enthusiastic receptions by the masses, and expressions of supreme adulation from the military and civil chiefs.

The peace reestablished, there was no basis for his continuation as provisional president, and on June 17th a decree was published calling for elections of members of congress and of the president of the Republic to be held on October 1st. The decree was accompanied by a recital of the achievements of the Liberal Party and of its great leader, Guzmán Blanco. For a while the country did not know whether Guzmán Blanco intended to leave the presidency, but all doubts were dissipated when *La Opinión Nacional*, the organ of his party, launched his candidacy for the presidency on August 1, 1872, and there was no opportunity for any opposition. The states were in the hands of military commanders appointed by Guzmán Blanco and when the only hope that he would fulfill the promise made many times of not seeking office disappeared, the result of the election was no longer in doubt.

The constitutional congress met on February 27, 1873, with Guzmán Blanco's father as president of the senate.

[15] *Ibid.*, p. 4.

On April 15th the popular vote was examined with the remarkable but, nevertheless, expected result that Guzmán Blanco received 239,691 votes; General Pulido, 9 votes; General Colina, 6 votes; while 3 solitary votes fell to the other three candidates. As vice presidents, in line with Guzmán Blanco's instructions, were elected generals Alcántara and Crespo against generals Pulido and Colina, who had greater claim to these offices because of their major contributions to Guzmán's victory. Subsequent events proved that the election of Alcántara and Crespo to the vice presidencies was a thoroughly premeditated step on Guzmán Blanco's part. In these two men he saw faithful followers whom he could elevate to the presidency after his term was over and on whom he could depend to serve his interests and to assure his return to the presidency when a decent interval between his constitutional periods in office allowed him to do so.

The years 1873 to 1877, constituting the four last years of the period known as the Septenio, were noteworthy for his efforts to build a personal following, for educational reforms, and for public works. It must be noted, however, that as far as the public works are concerned he explained the real purpose in his message to congress in 1877, when he said:

I have had to impress public expectation with a progress that would contain something of the extraordinary so that the disturbers of peace could not count on any sympathy whatsoever within the people. But this effort cannot be maintained as a permanent condition without causing great anxiety and without the possibility of a great and loud failure. On the other hand, since it is not necessary any more because public opinion has been formed and the revolutionaries have been fully discredited and rendered absolutely incompetent, I consider it more discreet to abandon in the future everything that is extraordinary and limit ourselves to preserving what has been done.[16]

[16] Hortensio, *Guzmán Blanco y su tiempo,* p. 250.

In this way, at the end of his seven-year rule, Guzmán disclosed the reasons for his engaging in extensive public works and in fostering material progress. He used these developments as a means to offset the unfavorable propaganda of the revolutionists and to accomplish this purpose he overextended his resources. He warned against the continuation of the same scope; first, because it was no longer necessary to counteract hostile propaganda, and second, because the lack of stability of such unsound development would jeopardize all that had been done heretofore.

Having completed the Septenio, Guzmán Blanco sought to secure his position by having General Alcántara as his successor to the presidency while he himself continued to feather his nest in Europe, where, as general representative of the Venezuelan government to a number of countries, he had the authority to negotiate contracts and loan agreements. The death of Alcántara, however, enabled elements opposed to Guzmán Blanco to gain control. This culminated in the demolition of Guzmán's statues, whereupon the much disgruntled envoy began to hatch revolutionary plans.

Guzmán played on the sympathy and desire for revenge of General Gregorio Cedeño, who felt that he should have been elected president instead of General Valera. Guzmán Blanco succeeded in influencing him to start a revolution against the Valera government. He also engaged from Paris in a voluminous correspondence with other generals. In a letter to General Carabano dated January 2, 1879, he wrote:

Although my intention was to retire completely from politics in Venezuela in order to live peacefully with my family, the latest events in Venezuela force me to concern myself again with the fate of the country. I believe that you should start a revolutionary movement in Guiana and also write to the presidents of the states of Barcelona and Maturín requesting them to take similar action.[17]

[17] *La reivindicación,* pp. 33–34.

While he repeatedly assured the country that he was no longer interested in office and professed his desire for peace, he suggests in this letter to General Carabano a number of steps to start a revolution in Venezuela.

The same date he wrote to General Pedro F. Sosa:

As I have no doubt that you are disposed to discharge your obligations for this cause, I limit myself to asking that you inspire General Carabano and persuade him of the glory which would ensue to him if Guiana, Apure, and El Guarico would unite to strengthen the salutary movement.[18]

In this letter, also, he incited General Sosa to initiate a revolutionary movement and sought his support in influencing General Carabano.

On January 3, 1879, he wrote to General Jacinto Lara:

I believe that patriotism forces me to take part in the struggle. I have left my retirement and I am unreservedly ready to act. I have sent to Crespo, Urbaneja, Acosta, and Pulgar 3,000 Remingtons with 500,000 rounds of ammunition and 10,000 precision rifles, and I will follow myself if Colina, Cedeño, or Carabano will call me.[19]

Claiming that his participation in the struggle was influenced by his interest in the country, he nevertheless advised General Lara that he had arranged shipment of substantial munitions to Venezuela to start a war.

On January 3, 1879, he also wrote to General Valera, the president of the republic, as follows:

What a dangerous situation it has fallen to your lot to preside over. What dangerous people, due to circumstances, have become your counselors. If I were not convinced of your liberalism and of your moderation, I would consider this letter useless, in spite of the importance that its sincerity gives it. In your place I would do

[18] *Ibid.*, p. 35.
[19] *Ibid.*, p. 45.

the following: I would convoke the plenipotentiaries of the twenty states; I would have it meet in Puerto Cabello so that it could be independent; and I would suggest to this congress that it name a provisional government which, instead of fanning the flame, would attempt to appease the various political groups and re-integrate the great Liberal Party, who are the liberals of the Septenio of first rank and with the best claims.

If you intend to follow this suggestion, don't consult with any-body. The people who surround you, without exception, are not concerned that you should come out well and with honor . . . if you think that I can be useful a cablegram will suffice. Don't think that I aspire to anything. I would return two or three months later, leaving you peaceful and happy. If you should want to ask advice of somebody, ask the Archbishop, Dr. Ponte.[20]

In this letter to General Valera, written in the familiar "thou," which is not translatable into English, Guzmán was at his best as the master plotter. First he warned Valera that he was surrounded by enemies. Then he tried to flatter him by stressing Valera's liberalism and moderation. Having made these two approaches, he concentrated on his main purpose and suggested, or almost ordered, how Valera should go about abolishing the existing government and establishing a new one composed of the true liberals of the seven-year regime of Guzmán Blanco. In conclusion he warned the president not to disclose this plan to his coun-selors. Should he want advice, Guzmán recommended that he consult the archbishop, Dr. Ponte.

On the same day, anticipating the possibility of a confer-ence between President Valera and Archbishop Ponte, he wrote the latter as follows:

Talk with General Valera, on whom it depends whether there will be a civil war, and publish a good pastoral letter advising that it be avoided. It is sufficient that the government of Caracas

[20] *Ibid.,* pp. 50–52.

appeal to the autonomy of the state, convoking a congress of plenipotentiaries in Puerto Cabello, in naming a provisional, intelligent, and very moderate government which would concern itself with the reintegration of the national party in the name of the Septenio. I promise you that in the new constitution we will declare that the Church is within a free state and that the state shall not have any religion except for the general supervision of all the religious cults. If Valera will render to the republic this immense service, the congress of plenipotentiaries should not adjourn without first granting him great honors and a large sum of money so that this exemplary citizen, who will have saved the republic from one of its major difficulties, can live well.[21]

Using the same familiar form of address, he wrote to Dr. Ponte, who owed his ascendancy to the post of Archbishop of Venezuela to Guzmán. He invoked his assistance in influencing President Valera to follow his wishes. He intimated that he would see to it that the new congress granted a substantial amount of money to Valera when he retired so that he could lead the life of an exemplary citizen and included in the letter bait for the archbishop himself, a promise that the new constitution which would be adopted would include a provision restoring to the Church considerable control.

In this manner, through exploiting the injured vanity of General Cedeño, through an appeal to the patriotism of General Carabano, through a deceptive letter to President Valera, and through a sanctimonious communication to Archbishop Ponte, Guzmán Blanco was moving the political and social forces in Venezuela while at the same time sending guns and ammunition and supplying the physical means for an insurrection and the outbreak of civil war.

His tactics were successful. President Valera rejected his request but the other generals responded to his appeal. Gen-

[21] *Ibid.*, pp. 52–53.

eral Cedeño headed the revolution. The government was not prepared to cope with it, and after several bloody battles, especially the one of February 6, 1879, when two thousand dead and over two thousand wounded were left on the field of combat at La Victoria, the road to Caracas was open.[22] Cedeño captured the city on February 13, 1879, and Guzmán Blanco was received on February 25, 1879, and assumed supreme command with the titles of Pacifier and Regenerator of Venezuela and Supreme Director of the Revindication.[23]

Having reestablished himself in power, Guzmán Blanco's activities were now turned, on one hand, toward punishing those who were responsible for the attacks against him and the demolition of his statues, and, on the other, toward designing a constitution that would insure the greatest concentration of power in his own hands and in the hands of his trusted followers. The federal Constitution of 1864, wherein great power was given to the individual states, was fashioned after the Constitution of the United States. Guzmán Blanco now decided that this form of constitution did not correspond to the realities of Venezuela and he switched to the Swiss model. The number of states were reduced from twenty to seven; a federal council consisting of one senator and two representatives from each of the seven states was formed; and the president was to be elected every two years from among the members of the federal council by the congress.[24]

This eliminated popular elections and concentrated both the legislative and the executive power in the hands of the representatives of the reduced states and their presidents, who were appointees of and dependent upon Guzmán Blanco.

[22] González Guinán, *Historia contemporánea de Venezuela*, XI, 21.
[23] *Ibid.*, XI, 32–33.
[24] *Ibid.*, XII, 304.

Although Guzmán Blanco was elected to a two-year term of presidency on March 13, 1880, the constitution was not ratified until April 11, 1881, and was not to take effect until February 20, 1882, so that his term of presidency could officially begin on February 20, 1882, and continue until 1884. By this maneuver, although elected in 1880 for a two-year term, he assured himself of retaining the presidency until 1884.

The two years of elective office, which stretched into five, from 1879 to 1884, ended with the elevation to the presidency of General Joaquín Crespo on April 27, 1884.[25] As in the case of Alcántara in 1878, Guzmán Blanco maneuvered the elections so that in spite of the fact that there were several more acceptable candidates, Guzmán Blanco's choice, General Crespo, was elected president of the republic.

After leaving the presidency to his friend, Crespo, Guzmán Blanco returned to Europe to bask in his glory as Venezuela's savior and to engage in social and financial activities. Again, as on the previous occasions, he assured Venezuela in his parting address that his mission had been fulfilled and he would not consider any entreaties to return and govern Venezuela. The same game, however, which had occurred many times previously, that of an appearance of public demand for the return of Guzmán Blanco, was put into operation the following year, in 1885. In February of that year his name appeared on the list of suggested presidential candidates. In spite of his seemingly magnanimous communication repudiating any call to office, he promptly forgot the fear of "soiling the glory of the Liberal Party and of sacrificing his reputation" and returned to Caracas on August 28, 1886, to reassume the presidency of Venezuela.[26]

During this term in office, known as the Bienio, he made

[25] *Ibid.*, XIII, 107.
[26] *Ibid.*, XIII, 353.

a serious attempt to consolidate his followers in order to avoid the repetition of the propaganda and attacks against him which followed every time he left his office and the country. Encouraged by these activities, his unconditional supporters suggested a change of the constitution so that he could continue in office. Overtly he frowned on the idea, but in 1887 he decided to sound out public opinion. When the experiment revealed, unpleasantly, a considerable element of opposition, he proceeded to imprison the editors and suspend the offending papers but did not dare to face the aroused public opinion by seeking another immediate term for himself. He again had to decide which of the several candidates would be most faithful to him.

Dissatisfied with General Crespo, whom he had promoted to the presidency in 1884, he placed his entire influence behind Dr. Rojas Paúl. To make it appear that he was allowing a free and uninfluenced election he turned over the presidency to General López and left Venezuela, but his arrangements had been completed and Rojas Paúl was elected to the presidency on July 2, 1888. His maneuver in promoting the candidacy of President Paúl, however, turned out to be his last decisive move in Venezuelan politics. Although raised to the presidency by Guzmán Blanco, Dr. Rojas Paúl seemed to be aware of the new challenges and movements in Venezuela. The press, no longer curbed by the repressive measures of Guzmán Blanco, resumed its campaign against him. Hostile symptoms began to appear also in congress, where Guzmán Blanco's contracts and negotiations carried on in Europe remained unapproved. President Paúl did not pay much attention to the extensive correspondence, advice, and proposals that Guzmán Blanco sent him from Paris, and soon the relations between the two reached the breaking point. Attempts on the part of Guzmán Blanco to meddle in the policies of Venezuela during the uprising of General

Crespo and to provoke unrest brought about a complete rupture of his relations with President Paúl. The latter refused to muzzle the critics of Guzmán Blanco and the agitation against him in Venezuela grew to such proportions that on the anniversary of the capture of Caracas by Guzmán Blanco, April 27th, the regular celebration of the day was transformed by the students and the people of Caracas into hostile demonstrations against Guzmán Blanco, which terminated in the destruction of his statues and monuments and in the sacking of his home. His era of influence and rule in Venezuela was definitely over.

CHAPTER VIII

ASPECTS OF A CAUDILLO REGIME:
THE UNQUALIFIED USE OF FORCE

THE DEGREE IN WHICH A RULER RESORTS to force and the manner in which he employs it are very largely a function of the conditions under which he seeks to maintain himself in power. Under the conditions prevailing in Venezuela during the period of Guzmán Blanco's rule, while there was a formal constitution and while lip service was paid to the principle of civil liberties, actually there existed throughout the country a continuous series of revolutionary movements, a state of affairs, indeed, that alternated between actual warfare and potential warfare. Under these conditions any man who possessed, or aspired to, power was either on your side or against you and might easily change his allegiance if his self-interest seemed to lie on the other side. Guzmán Blanco, consequently, was predisposed to look for signs of disaffection and to use strong measures to curb them. He might pay lip service to civil rights, but any dissentient voice was not only an offense to him personally but also a threat to a system of rule, under which discontent was the prelude to insurrection.

To show the manner in which Guzmán Blanco resorted to force and coercive activity we shall distinguish four periods in his regime. In the first period he was a member of the Falcón administration and acting president on many occasions and his primary interest was to amass a great fortune. A cornerstone in his fortune was the English loan and the means by which the loan was repaid. When he encountered a determined effort on the part of the domestic creditors, who had subscribed to a bond issue in 1861 and who had claimed their share of the customs-house income pledged to them at the time of the bond issue, Guzmán Blanco disposed of the petition submitted by them to the government by giving it the appearance of a hostile move on the part of the oligarchy, by forcing the Liberals to remove or disown their signatures on the memorandum, and by imprisoning five of the signers while others were hiding out in their homes or sought escape in flight to other countries. By use of his power in the government and by applying repressive measures, he succeeded in nullifying the just claims of the Venezuelan creditors and in protecting his share of income from the customs-house returns.[1]

During the second period, which included the military and political epoch of his successful fight against the Blue Revolution and the assumption of undisputed power in 1870, his coercive activities and repressive measures were directed with partial justification against some of his party's enemies who staged the attack on his home on August 14, 1869, and, in a much larger measure, against all actual and potential opponents. This was done in an attempt to crush all opposition to him, to suppress any critical expression against his regime, and to make it impossible for any group not only to rise in arms against him but to question his unlimited powers—in general, to strike terror into the heart of the people of Venezuela so as to assure himself of undisputed authority. In this period his wrath and repressive measures were directed not only against his enemies, but also against the members of his own party, against the generals who supported and led his revolutions, and even against the members of his own cabinet.

After occupying Caracas on April 27, 1870, he instituted

[1] Bigotte, *El libro de oro*, p. 83.

an intensive search and made wholesale arrests of the members of the Society of Santo Rosario whom he suspected of the attack on his home in August, 1869. Among the people who were hunted out and placed in the La Rotunda jail were many who did not belong to that society but who were considered opponents of the revolution.

His own instructions and comments indicated his determined repressive attitude. From Valencia on May 17, 1870, he writes to his ministers:

I am surprised that by the 14th there are not some ten or twelve additional prominent oligarchs arrested to accompany those I left imprisoned. The measures taken by General Escobar to prevent the exit from Caracas of the godos seem to me very good ones.[2]

Two years later, after the victory at Apure and the complete defeat of the opposition, he expresses the view that:

the matter of freeing the imprisoned or even of softening the repressive policy is one we cannot speak about as yet. The prisoners whom I have in La Guaira and in Caracas, those I have here [San Fernando], and those I shall continue to arrest here are a heavy charge but one indispensable to assure the peace of the republic.[3]

On February 4, 1872, in response to a memorandum of his cabinet which suggested that a large number of prisoners be freed on the occasion of the celebration of the victory of Apure, he comments:

I have already said from San Fernando that not one single detained person should be freed or given a passport for any reason whatsoever, notwithstanding the views expressed in the memorandum. I expect that the cabinet will carry out the following orders to the effect that any prisoner who has been freed should

[2] *Memorandum del General Guzmán Blanco,* p. 18.
[3] *Ibid.,* p. 240.

be returned to prison and anyone who has been given a passport should have it taken away from him and be forced to return to his previous residence.[4]

The printing house where *El Federalista*, the paper opposing him, was being published was taken as war booty and presented by his generals to Guzmán Blanco, who in turn made a personal gift of it to Vicente Coronado and Jesús María Soriano in recognition of their political services.[5] On May 12, 1870, he issued a decree seizing the properties of the high functionaries, military chiefs, and prominent members of the vanquished regime on the pretext that they were hiding or refused to recognize the triumph of the revolution. The seizure extended not only to the property of the individuals themselves, but to that of their families as well.[6] On May 14, while with his troops at Mariara, Guzmán Blanco ordered the further confiscation of the properties of conservative sympathizers in San Felipe, Guama, and Cocorote, as well as that of many others.[7] Upon his return to Caracas on May 30th of the same year, Guzmán Blanco, persisting in his repressive policies, issued another decree imposing contributions on the properties of all the individuals who in whatever manner disturbed the public order; providing further that in the case of the appearance of guerrillas in any part of the republic the properties, not only of the guerrillas but of all those who could be construed as the instigators of such uprisings, being seized and held by the state. He finally imposed a heavy contribution on many conservative partisans and on many others whose only guilt was the lack of the proper and enthusiastic reception of the triumph of the revolution.[8]

[4] *Ibid.*, p. 243.
[5] González Guinán, *Historia contemporánea de Venezuela*, IX, 386.
[6] *Recopilación de leyes*, V, 52.
[7] *Memorandum del General Guzmán Blanco*, pp. 14–15.
[8] *Ibid.*, p. 64.

His repressive measures did not stop with imprisonment, seizure of goods, and the levying of contributions. He unhesitatingly imposed and insisted on the death penalty. When on August 28, 1870, General Teodoro Carillo, a political prisoner in the La Rotunda jail, was murdered by the prison guards, Guzmán Blanco's comments were as follows:

The oligarchy is giving up in all points of the republic except in Caracas, and we must forget every other thing except to subjugate it through means of repression, including terror if necessary. It is possible that the death of Carillo will have a healthy influence on the fury of the prisoners. Otherwise, it represents nothing else but another corpse in this struggle.[9]

Another example of his attitude is presented in the following section of the *Memorandum:*

A new proof that our system is better is the arrest of Otazo and the death of Gamara. Because of this blow, it seems to me that there will be no other Otazo in the state of Bolívar who would want to become a guerrilla.[10]

His attitude to the members of his own army was no less severe. Although by December of 1871 the victory of his revolution was fully assured, he ordered the execution of chiefs accused of deserting. In the memorandum of December 8, 1871, he commanded: "The ministry should order General Espejo to bring the deserting chiefs before a council of war and execute them." [11] On December 24, 1871, he ordered:

Morales came with some thirty soldiers and with some twelve to fifteen chiefs and officers. The contingent from Tuy does not have even eighty soldiers. Salomé Pérez and at least one of the three officers who accompanied him in his desertion should be

⁹ *Recopilación de leyes,* V, 54.
¹⁰ *Memorandum del General Guzmán Blanco,* p. 134.
¹¹ *Ibid.,* p. 200.

shot, one in the Plaza de Cuys, the other in the Plaza de Ocumare. A similiar verdict should be carried out against General Vicente Marín, who should be shot at Santa Teresa.[12]

Guzmán Blanco's uncompromising attitude with regard to his generals has already been described in another section with reference to the case of General Salazar. On May 23, 1872, he defined his policy in such situations, stating:

The case of Espejo should be used to make a demonstration of our material power. It is not Espejo whom I want to subdue, but the reactionary spirit which continues latent in Caracas. I want to do everything on my part and take whatever precautions may be suggested so that it shall not be necessary to execute another Salazar.[13]

One of the achievements that Guzmán Blanco and the Liberal Party especially prided themselves on was the provision of the Constitution of 1864, amended by the congress in 1867, which provided for "the liberty of thought expressed by work or by the press, the latter without any restrictions. In case of offense, the injured one could bring his case before the tribunals of justice." [14]

In spite of this constitutional provision enacted by Guzmán Blanco and his Liberal Party, the period of his regime witnessed strict control over and continuous repressive measures against any publication in the press which did not follow his line or which dared to criticize any of his actions.

Dr. Modesto Urbaneja, a former member of the cabinet, was placed under arrest because he published one single paper entitled "The Actual Policy" in which, as a liberal, he criticized the policies of the government that in the name of the Liberal Party violated its doctrines.[15]

[12] *Ibid.*, p. 216.
[13] *Ibid.*, p. 307.
[14] Ruiz, *Historia patria,* p. 137.
[15] *Ibid.*, p. 203.

La Opinión Nacional, a newspaper which led the Venezuelan press in praising Guzmán Blanco, was suspended for three days because it dared to publish a statement by Father Sucre on the order of the minister exiling Archbishop Guevara.[16]

Because Pedro José Rojas, the man with whom Guzmán Blanco had signed the Treaty of Coche, had later fallen out with him over his financial deals, the liberal newspapers *El Eco de Carabobo* of Valencia and *El Siglo* XIX of Caracas were closed completely because they published a notice of Rojas's death.

The Caracas newspaper, *El Diario,* edited by Dr. Eduardo Calcano, was closed by the government because it stated in an editorial that the time had come for the return to the constitutional regime which had been offered by the president of the republic, Guzmán Blanco.

Strict censorship applied not only to opposition publications but also to the most loyal and favored publications. The editors and employees of *La Opinión Nacional* were threatened with exile because they published a telegram from Valencia without previous approval by the government. This censorship extended even to literary works which had no relation to politics. In a poetry contest in Caracas the poet Francisco G. Pardo was awarded the first prize for his ode on the "Power of the Idea." By the order of Guzmán Blanco, however, the prize was taken away from him because he did not eulogize the "Ilustre Americano"; it was cynically added in the order that the poet should get "an idea of power." [17]

The repressive measures extended not only to actual criticisms of the government but they also included philosophical and historical works which could be construed as veiled attacks on the government. Thus, Dr. Laureano Vil-

---

[16] *Ibid.,* p. 203.
[17] *Ibid.,* pp. 203–4.

lanueva, the editor of *El Demócrata,* was sent to jail and his newspaper was closed because he wrote a history on the usurpation of public power.[18]

Having disposed of his professed enemies and suspected opponents through death sentence, incarceration, or exile, Guzmán Blanco turned against the major military chiefs who supported him in the three-year struggle against the Blue Revolution, generals Ignacio Pulido and León Colina. When the congress met on March 10, 1874, General Pulido was not elected to the presidium of the congress because of the opposition of Guzmán Blanco and his support of General Alcántara. Pulido, on the eleventh, resigned his post as inspector general of the army. His resignation was accepted and was considered as a signal of his breaking with the policies of Guzmán Blanco. Guzmán Blanco immediately started a press campaign against him on the ground that Pulido was not the rightful possessor of some uncultivated lands for which the latter claimed to have paid in full. Pulido was being forced by the actions of Guzmán Blanco to defend himself which created a wider breach between the two of them and which resulted, as Guzmán Blanco anticipated, in an attempted revolt against him by General Pulido. This attempt gave Guzmán Blanco the excuse to launch a military campaign against Pulido, who was defeated and forced to flee the country.[19]

A similar situation was provoked by Guzmán Blanco against another possible pretender to the presidency, General Colina of Falcón's own state, Coro. Colina, smarting under the attitude of complete disregard shown to him by Guzmán Blanco, used his influence with the legislature of the state of Coro, and they came out on October 17, 1874, with a declaration against the authoritarian and tyrannical

---

[18] *Ibid.,* pp. 203–4.
[19] González Guinán, *Historia contemporánea de Venezuela,* X, 363–85.

regime of Guzmán Blanco. They particularly accused him of infringing upon the constitution, which provided for the sovereignty of the individual states, by placing the national army in the states, dictating elections, and arbitrarily selecting the president of the state and other officials. This act of the legislature gave Guzmán Blanco the opportunity of ordering his troops to march on Coro. Their campaign was successful. General Colina was defeated. Many of his supporters were jailed and Guzmán Blanco permanently disposed of two potential rivals to power.[20]

The third stage in the use of force occurred in 1879 when Guzmán Blanco was returned to power and began to settle accounts with the elements responsible for the public denunciations against him and for the demolition of his statues which occurred after he gave up the presidency at the end of the Septenio. Upon his return from France to Caracas in May 1879, Guzmán Blanco asked and received extraordinary authority (*facultades extraordinarias*) which he used to hunt out those who dared to voice criticism against his regime in the past. The events of 1870 of intensive search, wholesale, indiscriminate arrests, and confiscation of property and exile were repeated with greater energy. Not satisfied with his own repressive measures, Guzmán Blanco issued a statement to his sons (*lista para mis hijos*) in which he listed all of those whom he regarded as his personal enemies and entreated his sons to seek eternal vengeance against the opponents named in the list.[21]

This continuous specter of persecution provoked a number of states to rise against Guzmán Blanco and resulted in further bloodshed in the country. A number of attempts were made as well upon the life of Guzmán Blanco during the month of February, 1880. Through the information supplied

[20] *Ibid.*, X, 345.
[21] *Ibid.*, XII, 44.

by one of the conspirators, Guzmán Blanco succeeded in escaping death and in capturing General Abdon Otazo and fifteen other people who participated in the conspiracy. This attempt gave him further opportunity to impose restrictive measures upon the city of Caracas, which was seething with indignant recriminations against his use of force at a time when the country was at peace.[22]

Further revolutionary attempts occurred the same year, one being initiated by General Juan Machado who chartered a boat and sailed from the British isle of Trinidad to begin an insurrection in Venezuela on January 23rd.[23] Another attempt was made by General Natividad Solórzano, who was at one time chief of the cavalry guard of the president of the republic but was later peremptorily dismissed by Guzmán Blanco.[24] Both of these movements were suppressed by government troops. General Solorzano was captured and executed, but these attempts, as well as the conditions which provoked them, served to keep the country in continuous turmoil. On May 19, 1881, the congress extended the extraordinary authority given to Guzmán Blanco in 1880 and Guzmán Blanco continued to make effective use of the special prerogatives.

In 1881 General Gregorio Cedeño, the man who started the revolution of revindication in 1879 to bring Guzmán Blanco back to power, received his reward. Cedeño had hoped that after Guzmán Blanco had served a presidential term originally of two years, stretched ingeniously into five years, he would be a favored candidate of Guzmán Blanco for the presidency. The events of the first years of the Quinquenio convinced him that Guzmán Blanco was not considering him as a successor. Cedeño began then to organize

---

[22] *Ibid.*, XII, 171–80.
[23] *Ibid.*, XII, 223–39.
[24] *Ibid.*, XII, 261.

his own political following and started a campaign in the state of Carabobo. Guzmán Blanco, who could not openly attack him because of his past well-known services, succeeded in having him declared insane and committed.[25] The balance of his term in office in the Quinquenio was notable for a number of other minor uprisings, but with the elimination of generals Pulido, Colina, and Cedeño, there was no one left who could seriously contest his supremacy.

The fourth stage of his rule began with his return to office in 1886. During the first month of his two years in office, he declared himself in favor of the liberty of the press, hoping to win public approval by a surreptitious campaign, launched in the *Opinión Nacional,* for a change in the constitution that would enable him to seek another term in the presidency. This concession, however, was short-lived. When most of the newspapers bitterly attacked this attempt at usurpation of power, Guzmán Blanco had recourse to using his special authority. The newspapermen were jailed, the offending newspapers were closed, and Caracas was again the scene of indiscriminate arrests and intensive repressive measures.[26] It was on this note that Guzmán Blanco ended his rule of Venezuela in 1888.

[25] *Ibid.,* XII, 357.
[26] *Ibid.,* XIII, 489.

CHAPTER IX

ASPECTS OF A CAUDILLO REGIME:

FINANCIAL CHICANERY

THROUGHOUT HIS ENTIRE CAREER one of Guzmán Blanco's primary concerns was to amass a personal fortune. While it is undoubtedly true that under his government Venezuela showed remarkable economic progress, it is difficult to draw the line between the financial transactions which Guzmán Blanco made for the benefit of Venezuela and those which he made for his own profit. His name or the names of the members of his immediate family were associated with almost every economic enterprise in Venezuela, whether of public or private character, throughout his administration. He personally participated in the negotiations and arrangements for the international loans made to Venezuela and his several periods of administration were studded with concessions and grants made to the members of his family in the construction of roads, in the building of the aqueducts and sewage systems, in the erection of government buildings, and even in the field of agricultural production and distribution.

Guzmán Blanco's drive to attain great wealth began as early as 1863, while he was one of the leaders of the federal revolution under Falcón. His advocacy of the Treaty of Coche, which terminated the Federal War, was influenced by an understanding made with Dr. Pedro Rojas, the secretary general of the Páez government. At Coche, Dr. Pedro José Rojas showed Guzmán Blanco the secrets of the treasury of Venezuela and the means of enriching himself through the advocacy of contracted and pending loans. It developed that on July 31, 1862, Dr. Hilarion Nadal, the fiscal commissioner of Venezuela, had completed negotiations for a loan with Baring Brothers of London.[1] The nominal amount of the loan was to be £1,000,000, but the actual cash to be realized on it amounted to £630,000.[2] The interest was to be 6 percent per annum on the total nominal amount of £1,000,000, payable the first of May and the first of November of each year. The loan was to be amortized annually at the rate of 2 percent of the nominal capital.[3]

At the same time the Venezuelan government asked Baring Brothers to capitalize a further loan of £214,000, which represented the amount of unpaid interest for four semesters due to foreign holders of Venezuelan bonds, and also agreed to pay 6 percent interest on this additional amount.[4]

The payment of the amortization and of the interest was to be guaranteed by a mortgage on 55 percent of the import duties to be obtained in the customs houses of La Guaira and Puerto Cabello, estimated to render at least £164,000 annually. This 55 percent was to be delivered to an agent or agents designated by Baring Brothers. Should the amount of 55 percent exceed the interest and amortization charges, the balance was to be applied toward further amortization of the loans.[5]

Baring Brothers, on their part, obligated themselves upon completion of the subscription of the loans to pay the interest which was due to the owners of Venezuelan bonds for four semesters, until July 1, 1862, and pay also £60,000, which would represent the interest of the first two semesters on the total nominal loan of £1,000,000. They were to retain £15,000, which they claimed was owed to them by the

---

[1] *A Letter . . . by Messrs. Baring Brothers*, pp. 26–27.
[2] *Ibid.*, p. 28.
[3] *Ibid.*, p. 28.
[4] *Ibid.*, p. 29.
[5] *Ibid.*, p. 31.

government of Venezuela, and £12,500 as commission for carrying through the deal and were to pay the rest of the money to the government of Venezuela, who was supposed to use it to reinstate the circulation of hard currency in the country.[6]

On September 9, 1862, Mr. E. Mocatta, the representative of Baring Brothers, called on Secretary General Rojas in the company of the British Chargé d'Affaires Orme and advised him that Baring Brothers had placed the loan on the London Exchange and there were good chances for the subscription.[7] On November 1, 1862, General Páez ratified this loan.[8]

After approving the loan, the government of Venezuela issued two decrees offering to pay 75 percent of the nominal value of the paper money issued by the Bank of Venezuela, which had ceased to exist, and also offering to pay 40 percent of the nominal value of ordinary shares which had been issued by the Bank of Venezuela. These payments and conditions were arranged in accordance with the specified periods when Venezuela was supposed to obtain the monies realized from the approved loan. A special institution, under the name of Banco de Caracas, was established to handle the liquidation and exchange of the instruments and Messrs. Carlos Hahn and Giacomo Servadio were named as directors.[9]

Giacomo Servadio, one of the two directors, was a close friend and business associate of Secretary General Rojas, and presumably Rojas shared with Servadio in the proceeds of the management of the financial transactions in Venezuela and the relationship with Baring Brothers.

Antonio Guzmán Blanco met Dr. Rojas at Coche on April 23, 1863, barely six months after the Baring Brothers loan

[6] *Ibid.*, p. 30.
[7] *Ibid.*, p. 11.
[8] *Recopilación de leyes*, IV, 188.
[9] González Guinán, *Historia contemporánea de Venezuela*, VIII, 41.

was approved, and the benefits accrued by Rojas and Servadio could be easily demonstrated. Rojas, realizing that the federation forces under Falcón would be victorious, was concerned first as to whether Falcón's government would continue to honor Venezuela's obligations under the loan; secondly, Rojas was anxious to retain control over the 55 percent income from the customs houses; and thirdly, he wanted to participate in the profits that might come from a new loan of one million pounds for which his business associate, Giacomo Servadio, had begun negotiations in London early in 1863 through Mattison and Company.[10] There is no doubt that these facts were revealed to, and influenced, Guzmán Blanco. In the first place, immediately after the signing of the Treaty of Coche and the entry of Falcón into Caracas, Guzmán began to advocate negotiations for a loan from England. Secondly, after Falcón formed his government, he took over the ministry of foreign relations and treasury so as to have jurisdiction over the customs houses and the incomes derived therefrom. Thirdly, he sought and obtained a commission to go to England to negotiate a loan. Fourth, upon arriving in England, he immediately contacted and used the services of Giacomo Servadio, since he himself knew no English and was not acquainted with the financial situation in London.

Guzmán Blanco's personal interest in the loan contracted for under the dictatorship was expressed in later years through his efforts to control the import duties at La Guaira and Puerto Cabello; he did this under the pretext of protecting the 55 percent of the income which was earmarked for payment of the loan contracted for through Baring Brothers. One of his steps upon taking over the executive power during one of the many absences of Falcón from Caracas was to make a contract with Alejandro Viso, by virtue of which

[10] Briceño, *Los ilustres,* p. 62.

Viso was to furnish the general treasury with 5,000 pesos daily against the payments of the customs houses at La Guaira and receive the accepted discount.[11]

Guzmán Blanco was an associate of Viso's in this business, but Viso, instead of delivering to the treasury the 5,000 daily pesos, began to buy up payment orders, pensions, and other invoices upon the treasury. He bought these at a lower price than their face value but charged the full value to the treasury when making his accounts. The profit derived from these transactions was considerable. When, after a while, Guzmán Blanco began to suspect that his associate was not giving him the proper share of the returns, he had him jailed. Not satisfied with merely putting his associate into prison, Guzmán Blanco sent two of his trusted men, Diego Urbaneja and José Aurrecoechea, to visit him in jail and demand under pain of physical punishment repayment of the sum which Guzmán Blanco considered due him. When Viso first refused he was given a severe beating by Aurrecoechea and was forced to issue a check on the Banco Británico. The next morning Guzmán Blanco's brother-in-law, Luis Villenilla, presented the check at the bank and after it was duly paid Viso was released from prison. It was estimated that on this transaction alone Guzmán Blanco made approximately 220,000 pesos in the period from November, 1864, to June, 1876.[12]

The second incident with regard to the 55 percent import duty deserves notice as it also represents the manner in which Guzmán Blanco handled the funds of the treasury. In 1861, under the dictatorship, a loan, known as Billetes of January 15, 1861, was floated which was subscribed internally and was guaranteed by 38 percent of the returns of the customs houses. When the subsequent loan of the dictatorship, con-

[11] Ibid., p. 82.
[12] Bigotte, El libro de oro, pp. 54–55.

tracted with Baring Brothers on November 1st, imposed a mortgage of 55 percent of the duties collected at the customs houses, there arose a dispute between the internal creditors and the English creditors which came to a head while the Falcón regime was in power. Two conferences were called on November 19th and on November 29th, 1864, by the ministry of hacienda which was headed by Guzmán Blanco. Since no agreement was arrived at during these conferences, the matter was referred by Guzmán Blanco to the federal supreme court and in the meantime Guzmán Blanco ordered that the 55 percent should be deposited with the treasury until a final decision could be made on the matter. Guzmán Blanco asked the opinion of the supreme court on these two points:

1. How does the previous mortgage influence the right of the mortgagors?

2. On consideration of the case, which of the two mortgagor creditors has the preference?

The court ruled in favor of the domestic creditors, but Guzmán Blanco, who wanted to retain control and manage the proceeds of the customs houses, began a double game by telling the internal creditors that the proceeds of the customs houses must be used to pay Baring Brothers in order to protect the good name of Venezuela abroad and, in turn, by telling Baring Brothers that he was looking for a means of reaching a suitable agreement with the privileged creditors who were upheld by the decision of the supreme court.[13]

To make certain of the continuity of effort, he sent his father, Antonio Leocadio Guzmán, to London to act as minister of Venezuela and present the case there in the way that the son was presenting it in Caracas. When the *Morning*

[13] *A Letter . . . by Messrs. Baring Brothers,* Appendix 5.

Chronicle of London, which took Guzmán Blanco's state-
ments seriously, attacked the Venezuelan creditors as being
responsible for payments withheld from the English subscribers of the dictatorship loan, the Venezuelan creditors
presented a petition to the government asking for justice;
on the one hand, their claims recognized by the supreme
court were not met and, on the other hand, their reputation
was ruined abroad. Guzmán Blanco arrested most of the
signers of the petition and forced the others to flee the
country.[14]

There are various accounts of the profit that accrued to
Guzmán Blanco by retaining in trust the 55 percent of the
proceeds of the customs houses. According to treasury reports, the collections of import duties at the La Guaira customs house from November, 1864, to June, 1865, amounted
to $1,860,329. The income at Puerto Cabello for the same
period amounted to $1,550,706. The total collections for the
two customs houses amounted to over $2,862,000[15] and 55
percent of this total sum, which was over $1,574,000, was
retained in trust by Guzmán Blanco but never accounted for.

The second important financial transaction, which produced as many repercussions as the Baring Brothers loan
and which also enriched Guzmán Blanco to the same degree,
was the loan negotiated by him personally in the fall of 1863.
On August 8, 1863, Guzmán Blanco went to London as the
fiscal representative of the Falcón government with the
authority and instructions issued to him by the president and
the cabinet on August 6th, and presumably written by him
while he held the post of secretary of the treasury. The presidential order and instructions authorized him to make a
loan up to £2,000,000 sterling at the most favorable rate of

---

[14] Bigotte, *El libro de oro*, pp. 68–83.
[15] *Memoria de Hacienda, 1866*, Document 2.

interest and conditions with the right to mortgage import duties at La Guaira and Puerto Cabello or any other national properties.[16]

Armed with this authorization, Guzmán Blanco arrived in London. His first step was to reject negotiations for a loan of £1,000,000 which Servadio had initiated with Mattison and Company. He considered the amount too small. With the cooperation of this same Servadio he entered into negotiations with the London Company of Credit and Finance, represented by Mr. Thomas McDonald and Company, and concluded an agreement with him to float a loan of £1,500,000 sterling at 60 percent of the face value, with 6 percent interest and 2 percent amortization. To repay the loan and the interest, he offered a mortgage on the export duties of the customs houses at La Guaira, Puerto Cabello, Maracaibo, and Ciudad Bolívar and also the import duties of all the customs houses if the export duties should not suffice to cover the annual obligations.[17] This additional mortgaging of the income from the import duties was made in spite of two outstanding mortgages on the import duties at La Guaira and Puerto Cabello, the one of 38 percent held by the internal subscribers of the January 15, 1861, loan, and the second of 55 percent held by Baring Brothers to guarantee the £1,000,000 loan entered into on November 1, 1862.

Guzmán Blanco returned to Venezuela on November 23rd with the project of the loan. Considerable opposition to the project had developed and for a while Falcón himself faltered in the support of Guzmán Blanco. Thanks, however, to the aid of General Jacinto Pachano, the brother-in-law of Falcón, who finally swayed Falcón to Guzmán Blanco's side, and to the maneuvering of his father, Antonio Leocadio Guzmán, who was the president of the congress which met in January

[16] *Memoria de Hacienda, 1865*, p. 39.
[17] *Ibid.*, pp. 40–42.

of 1864 and which considered the loan, and to Guzmán Blanco's own lobbying with the members of the congress the loan was approved on January 14, 1864.[18] Guzmán Blanco, now accompanied by Jacinto Pachano, returned to London in February, 1864, to complete the arrangements for the loan.

The sale of the bonds was launched in London in April in denominations of 500, 200, and 100 pounds.[19] In spite of the very advantageous terms to the subscribers, however, and although the original negotiations were for £1,500,000, Venezuela's low credit standing made it impossible to obtain subscriptions for more than £428,500 by the English company.[20]

Since so partial a result would have not only impaired Guzmán Blanco's prestige as a financial emissary but also would have deprived him of the commission on the unissued amount of the loan, he entered into an agreement with Servadio, who took over bonds for £500,000, and Guzmán Blanco himself retained, for the time being, the unsubscribed bonds of £571,500.[21]

Servadio did not have the money to pay for these bonds, but he and Guzmán Blanco were able to arrive at a rather ingenious agreement. As the actual cash returns on the loan were only 60 percent, by subscribing to £500,000 and deducting 6 percent interest he was responsible for only £270,000.[22] From this £270,000 he deducted 5 percent commission payable to Guzmán Blanco, or £25,000, and 2 percent amortization for one year, or £10,000, making a total of £35,000 and leaving an amount due of £100,000 which was owed him from the loan of the Páez government.[23]

[18] *Ibid.*, pp. 44–45.
[19] *Evening Star* of London, April 14, 1864, quoted by Level de Goda in *Historia contemporánea de Venezuela política y militar*, pp. 606–7.
[20] *Memoria de Hacienda, 1865*, p. 59.
[21] *Ibid.*, p. 60.
[22] *Ibid.*, p. 60.
[23] *Ibid.*, p. 61.

Servadio was also credited with the net balance of £51,700 on an additional £110,000 par value bonds given to him by Guzmán Blanco to liquidate further indebtedness on the export duties (£110,000, less 40 percent discount, less 6 percent interest for one year, less 2 percent amortization for one year, less 5 percent commission to Guzmán). This meant that in the final accounting Servadio had only paid £83,300 (£235,000, less £151,700) for bonds of a total face value of £500,000.[24]

A similarly ingenious method was used by Guzmán Blanco to dispose of the bonds worth £571,500, which he retained. As soon as word that the loan was open for subscription reached Venezuela, General Trias, who was then acting president for Falcón, made a number of demands for money on Guzmán Blanco. Realizing that the £428,500 which were subscribed through the English company would in reality yield only £201,160 (60 percent of £428,500 less £55,640 to cover Guzmán Blanco's 5 percent commission, the advance annual interest of 6 percent and the advance annual amortization of 2 percent), Guzmán Blanco made an effort to obtain additional cash. He entered into an agreement with the W. Morgan Company for a loan of £120,000, offering as security bonds with a face value of £400,000.[25] On this £120,000 he paid a 10 percent commission, which reduced the loan to £108,000 and from this he deducted for himself a commission of 5 percent on the £400,000 worth of bonds placed as security, leaving a net for Venezuela of £88,000.

There are many versions as to the actual profit Guzmán

[24] *Ibid.*, p. 61. Level de Goda, in *Historia política y militar de Venezuela*, claims that Servadio deducted from the £235,000 the amount of £162,705 due on the Páez loan and £67,107 due on the Kennedy loan, which meant that he had only to pay £5,188 for bonds having a nominal value of £500,000 (pp. 609–10).

[25] *Ibid.*, p. 62.

Blanco realized on this transaction which placed the heavy obligation of £1,500,000 on Venezuela; at the rate of exchange then in effect it amounted to 9,750,000 pesos, out of which the government received in actual cash only about 2,300,000 pesos or less than 25 percent of the obligation assumed. Guzmán Blanco himself admitted to receiving 5 percent on the full face value of the loan; i.e., £75,000 or, including expenses, over 500,000 pesos.[26]

It is interesting to note that having negotiated the loan and having obtained his commission, Guzmán was not greatly concerned about repaying either interest or amortization. On July 2, 1866, payment of interest on the loan of 1864 was suspended. Payment was renewed in 1866 but it finally stopped in 1867.[27]

These financial dealings cover the period of Guzmán Blanco's temporary elevation to power during the Federal War and during the regime of Marshal Juan Falcón. His handling of government money and his conduct of national and private business affairs during the years when he was the undisputed master of Venezuela was no less subject to question. On the whole, they did not provoke the same scandal as did the Baring Brothers deal or the loan of the federation because, as the supreme master of Venezuela who did not require the approval of a Falcón, he was able to keep his actions more secret.

During the Septenio he relied on his minister of development, Dr. José María Rojas, to negotiate the large contracts for public works, most of which were, surprisingly, given out to General Juan Francisco Pérez, Luis Oduber, and H. L. Boulton and Company, all business associates of Guzmán

[26] *Ibid.*, pp. 49–50.
[27] Eastwick, *Sketches of Life in a South American Republic with the History of the Loan of 1864*, pp. 119–22.

Blanco. The large contracts for public works required the approval of congress but, on the whole, no one dared oppose Guzmán Blanco or question his arrangements.

On August 25, 1873, and on January 2, 1874, Dr. José María Rojas made a contract with General Juan Francisco Pérez to establish a steamship line between La Guaira and Nutrias. This contract was approved by the congress at its session of June 6, 1874,[28] as was also another made with the same General Pérez for a submarine telegraph line from La Guaira to Port of Spain, Trinidad.[29] On the same day, June 6th, congress approved a contract given out to Luis Oduber for building a lighthouse on the island of Gran Roque.[30]

Francisco Fossi and Antonio Aranguren were given the exclusive monopoly for steamship navigation on the lakes of Maracaibo in 1874,[31] and this concession also resulted in their gaining a complete monopoly on the importation of flour into Venezuela. On June 14, 1867, H. L. Boulton and Company was given the commission to introduce nickel money into Venezuela and arrangements to mint the money in the United States for the value of 150,000 venezolanos were entrusted to them. The nickel coins were delivered to Venezuela and placed in circulation about the time when Guzmán Blanco left the presidency in 1877. Since this was a more easily verifiable transaction and since Guzmán was no longer in power, the Boulton company was accused of not minting the right proportion of nickel and Guzmán Blanco was attacked for indiscriminately paying out 150,000 venezolanos.[32] The minister of the treasury in the subsequent regime of General Alcántara investigated and confirmed

---

[28] *Actos legislativos*, p. 215.
[29] *Ibid.*, p. 222.
[30] *Ibid.*, p. 224.
[31] *Ibid.*, p. 212.
[32] González Guinán, *Historia contemporánea de Venezuela*, XI, 290–92.

these charges, to which Guzmán Blanco answered in a letter to General Aristeguieta:

Nickel! Oh, what infamy! Would a man who has millions prostitute himself to the point of stealing cents from the public treasury? [33]

The second charge made against Guzmán Blanco after he left the presidency in 1878 came, strangely enough, from his uncle-in-law, Dr. Modesto Urbaneja. In a pamphlet entitled *Notes on the Contract Entered into in Paris by Dr. José María Rojas and Mr. José María Antomarche Herreros for the Construction of a Railroad between La Guaira and Caracas,* Dr. Urbaneja charged that the financial arrangements were injurious to Venezuela, that the charges made by the construction company were exorbitant, and that there were apparently other motives which influenced Dr. Rojas to enter into this contract made during the administration of Guzmán Blanco. On June 4, 1878, a special commission was appointed by the minister of public works to examine the terms of the contract, and on June 26th, acting on the recommendation of the commission, the contract was canceled.[34] There is no record that Guzmán Blanco protested the cancellation of this contract which apparently, unlike the nickel transaction, was not big enough to merit his personal attention.

The following year Guzmán Blanco was out of power; but he came back to Venezuela in April, 1879, after the success of the Revolution of Revindication which returned him to power. On May 7, 1879, a new contract was issued for the construction of the railroad from La Guaira to Caracas, this time with Charles J. Brandman who was also given a contract on the same day to build a railroad between Valencia and Puerto Cabello.[35]

[33] Quoted by Briceño, *Los ilustres,* p. 159.
[34] González Guinán, *Historia contemporánea de Venezuela,* XI, 306.
[35] *Recopilación de leyes,* VIII, 195–96.

Having resumed power, Guzmán Blanco returned to Paris ostensibly to bring his family back to Venezuela, but while he was there his former minister of development, Dr. José María Rojas, who was now the fiscal representative of Venezuela in Europe, began negotiations with the French banker, Eugenio Rodríguez Pereire, for a transaction of truly colossal proportions.

Under the pretext that he was inspired by Guzmán Blanco's desire to accelerate the exploitation of the natural resources of Venezuela, Dr. Rojas negotiated with M. Pereire for the establishment of a great industrial company which would be given the following concessions:

1. All uncultivated lands to be delivered to the company to make a place for foreign colonization.

2. The concession for all the coal deposits of the nation with a provision for compensation on the net products.

3. The concession for all the fertilizers and phosphates of which the nation could dispose.

4. Authorization to establish a mint in Caracas or in Ciudad Bolívar to coin the metals which the country would produce.

5. The concession for placing a submarine cable to the Antilles islands.

6. Rights of preference over all the mining resources of the nation.

7. Exclusive concessions for steam navigation of the rivers Orinoco, Apure, Portuguesa, Aruca, and other navigable ways, as well as the lakes of Maracaibo and Valencia and the canal of the river Tuy. These concessions also included the postal service on these boats.

8. Preferential authorization to build railroads, street cars, and highways.

9. The concession to exploit the forests of the territory of Amazonas and others.

10. The concession for the exploitation of quinine.

11. The right to issue obligations in shares as it was done by the city of Paris.

12. Authorization to establish warehouses, public markets, and sales places and to issue negotiable instruments.

13. Authorization to manufacture dynamite and other explosive products.

14. The concession to colonize the islands of the Colón territory.

15. The concession to establish in Venezuela a central clearing house of immigration from all the countries.

16. The right to transfer some concessions with the previous agreement of the Venezuelan government.[36]

Guzmán Blanco wisely remained in Paris, but his representative, Dr. José María Rojas, and the representative of Pereire, Theodore Delort, arrived in Caracas in September and met with the united opposition of the country and the cabinet, which had been apprised of the terms of the contract by the newspapers of September 27th. Delort returned to Paris firmly convinced that the Venezuelan public opinion was definitely opposed to the agreement. No further action was taken and the grandiose plan for the exploitation of Venezuela by a foreign syndicate was abandoned.

During the Quinquenio, or five-year administration, Guzmán Blanco continued with his construction of railroads, but since Charles Brandman, with whom he made an agreement on May 5, 1879, defaulted, he turned to an American promoter, W. A. Pile, and entered into an agreement with him

---

[36] González Guinán, *Historia contemporánea de Venezuela,* XII, 120–22.

on October 22, 1880, for the construction of the railroad from La Guaira to Caracas and from Puerto Cabello to Valencia financed through foreign bonds. This initiated the practice of foreign finance of the railroads and as a result the road from La Guaira to Caracas, as well as the others constructed thereafter, became the property of foreign shareholders.

Guzmán Blanco returned to power again in 1886, after an interval of two years, and held the office of the presidency of Venezuela from 1886 to 1888. In the latter part of 1887, as his parting gesture in leaving the government, he issued a number of decrees and contracts, among them a contract with the governor of the federal district and Guzmán Blanco's son-in-law, Morny, to provide the piping for the aqueduct of Macarao which supplied the city of Caracas.[37]

Upon retiring from office, Guzmán Blanco proceeded to Paris as minister plenipotentiary of Venezuela and with the authority to negotiate financial agreements and contracts of public works for Venezuela. This was the reward given to him by President Rojas Paúl whom he supported against General Crespo. Guzmán Blanco, however, never capitalized on this reward. Subsequent political events turned President Paúl against him and when innumerable contracts and financial proposals sent by Guzmán Blanco from Paris did not receive the attention of President Paúl and were not approved by congress, the relations between President Paúl and Guzmán Blanco were ended, as was also the latter's role in the manipulation of the finances of Venezuela.

[37] *Ibid.,* XIII, 582–83.

CHAPTER X

Aspects of a Caudillo Regime: Personalism

Persistently evident in all the relationships and actions of Guzmán Blanco, characteristically alike in his way of thinking and his way of ruling, is the trait of personalism. It is the caudillo's response to his situation and though the response may take a variety of expressions it is inevitably permeated by an essential common quality that is hard to define but not difficult to recognize. It reveals the nature of the bond between a type of autocratic ruler and all the individuals and groups with whom he comes in contact directly or indirectly. Guzmán Blanco exhibited this trait in a manner that changed somewhat from time to time, responsive to his changing hold on power. Before showing some of its manifestations, however, we shall try to distinguish the type of authority exercised by a ruler such as Guzmán Blanco from that of other kinds of rulers.

According to Max Weber, the authority to rule depends on one or the other of three forms of legitimacy, rational, traditional, and charismatic.[1]

Rational legitimacy. Here authority is based on fundamental laws and on recognized legal regulations. The right to exercise it is formulated in precise terms; jurisdiction is defined. Authority is, in other words, interpreted functionally. The rules that define it are "rationally" devised and established so as to assure the fulfillment of an official function. Weber thinks of this type of government as preeminently of

[1] Weber, *Wirtschaft und Gesellschaft*, pp. 17 ff.

bureaucratic structure. Within it the relation of the ruler to the people and the acceptance by the people of his right to rule is primarily impersonal. An example of this type would be the elective president of a republic.

Traditional legitimacy. Here authority is rendered legitimate by the sanction of the established ways. This is the oldest ground of authority, and systems based upon it have predominated throughout history. The institution of power is integrally bound up with the customs of the people. There are various traditionally determined systems in accordance with which authority is transmitted from generation to generation. A patriarchal order, an oriental dynasty, a feudal order, or a modern monarchy would alike be examples of this traditional legitimacy. Such systems may be given a legal structure but the law merely reflects a tradition that is uppermost, not the rationality of the order of things.

Charismatic legitimacy. In the third type of legitimacy the ruler or leader is the "anointed one," the man apart, endowed with extraordinary attributes that distinguish him sharply in the eyes of his followers or subjects from the run of men. In the religious sphere he is the "prophet." In the secular world he is the man with a mission, sometimes the man ordained of God, at least the man of destiny. He has an appeal that makes him the focus of a devoted band of followers. In times of crisis he emerges as the deliverer, the champion of the people. He is the man who symbolizes the aspirations of his people, or at least of a majority of them. He rules by his personal magnetism. Always he appears in the name of some great cause. In a sense he incarnates the cause and this fact legitimatizes his power. The modern dictator in effect claims this kind of charisma in the stage of his achievement of power and seeks thereafter to convey the impression that he is the permanent possessor of it.

We should understand that these three types are not

clearly separate. A particular ruler may possess some elements of two or of all three of them. The point is that one or another is the major ground of authority in the eyes of the people. It is evident, however, that no one of Weber's three types or any combination of them can be applied to the rule of Guzmán Blanco. The basis of his authority, in other words, was precarious. He did not possess traditional legitimacy since there was no established line of succession to power by inheritance or by other rights of which his rule was the expression. Nor could he justly claim to be the bearer of rational legitimacy. He was not a constitutional ruler, operating within the limits of and subject to the controls of a system defined by law. Whatever principles he professed at one time or another he proceeded to violate without scruple. He won and retained office by stratagem and chicanery, and the elections held during his regime were the merest façade. There remains, then, only charismatic legitimacy, and while his speeches and those of his friends often pictured him as the savior of his country and the man of destiny, the claim was too meretricious, too much a mask for self-seeking ambition. He embodied no particular cause. He had no outstanding quality that won the veneration or even the lasting devotion of a band of disciples. He had no charisma.

The lack of any sure ground of legitimacy means that the ruler must try to compensate for it in one way or another. He puts forward, for example, spurious claims to legitimacy, and his claims are the louder and the more rhetorical because he tries to conceal their hollowness. This characteristic is evident in the speeches and proclamations of Guzmán Blanco. He must magnify his personal services, his personal qualities, and the peculiar need of the country for him and for him alone. He is, nevertheless, insecure and he must, therefore, resort to any stratagems and any use of power, however arbitrary, that will crush nascent opposition. He cannot afford to abide by any constitutional principles. He must eliminate opponents whom he cannot conciliate or bribe. Guzmán Blanco's rise to power, his maintenance of himself in power, and even his final loss of power followed this caudillo pattern in which personalistic claims and attributes become the all-sufficient forms of the regime. In the case of Guzmán Blanco this pattern expresses itself in three main stages. In the first stage, the bid for power in his own right, Guzmán Blanco depended upon his bold, authoritative gesture as the man of prestige and experience who claimed the ability to rescue Venezuela from the anarchy and internal collapse brought about by the Blue Revolution and the subsequent struggle between conservatives and liberals. His turbulent restlessness while in opposition, his ability to draw upon himself the concentrated hatred of the conservatives and the lynchers of Santa Rosalia, his bold and presumptuous challenge of the existing order in the name of the liberal cause, and the heroic appeal inspired by the exaggeration of his exploits in the Federal War influenced and gained for him political malcontents, budding caudillos, ambitious bureaucrats, beguiled intellectuals, and resurgent masses. Exploiting to the full his fame as a beneficent administrator, which he created for himself during the Falcón regime, playing upon regional antagonisms and personal rivalries, holding out the promise of spoils and a share of power, and moving the masses by his dramatic actions and passionate speeches, he succeeded in winning the acceptance of his authority and leadership. He was placed at the head of a successful insurrection which brought him to supreme power in the country in April of 1870.

In the second stage, the time of entrenchment in power, there was even greater personalist emphasis. When power fell into the hands of Guzmán Blanco the idea of the state became identified with the doctrines of the Liberal Party, the doctrines of the latter with the tendencies of the government, and the government with the views and wishes of Guzmán Blanco, who considered all those who were not in complete agreement with him as enemies of the Fatherland. His strength was supposed to derive from the Liberal Party whose leader and spokesman he professed to be, but as if in retribution for the insincere preoccupation with the political structure of the nation, his Liberal Party had little actual strength and a minimum of formal organization. Because he found it necessary to emphasize his interests and his will as guiding principles at all times, perverting to that end the policies and slogans of the Liberal Party, he could not afford to create an organization among his followers that might have been taken by them as a legitimate organ and used to limit his prerogatives and activities in any way.

The people who actually kept him in office and on whose support he could rely consisted of elements whose main source of solidarity was personal allegiance to him. They were his kin, primarily his father, Antonio Leocadio Guzmán, who used his prestige and influence to spread the right kind of propaganda through the press, acting also as his spokesman for the Liberal Party and carrying the brunt of his legislative maneuvers during the sessions of congress; local caudillos and minor military chieftains who, through his favor, attained the presidency of particular states or the military command of regions; the associates of his family and his close business acquaintances, whose fortunes were directly dependent upon his success, together with those who indirectly expected to benefit from his rule because of the money freely spent on public works and large contracts; and feudal overlords who were attached to him because of the regime of peace and order he was expected to impose.

In addition to this temporarily dominant and always fluctuating elite, there were the relatively inert masses who had no knowledge, no voice, and no power. They acquiesced to autocratic domination and could be easily aroused to the heights of enthusiasm and adoration but could be similarly swayed, sooner or later, to resentment and revolt, to the demolition of statues and the sacking of homes.

While we say that Guzmán Blanco came to depend on these elements for his power and domination, his attitude toward them did not indicate any recognition of obligation or any sense of appreciation of their unqualified support. The only exception was his father, whom he attempted to glorify as the Father of the Country and as a collaborator of Bolívar so that added prestige could be attached to his own name.

His manner of dealing with his cabinet ministers was curt and arrogant. The memorandum, which includes his correspondence with his cabinet from May 12, 1870, to July 31, 1872, is replete with abusive remarks, sarcastic criticisms, and insolent instructions.

I do only what I want and everybody should know it.

I neither want nor like ministers who think. I want only ministers who can write, because the only one who can think am I, and the only one who does think am I.[2]

His attitude toward the caudillos and military chieftains who returned him to power on several occasions was no less arbitrary and negative. In the memorandum he characterized General Monserrate as a drunkard, General Benítez as a thief, and General Colina as a beast. He did not stop, however, with these appellations. He took steps to eliminate those whom he felt to be potential threats to his personal power.

An essential aspect of this stage was his ruthless crushing of opposition and use of terror, his cunning manipulation or

---

[2] Luis Gerónimo Alfonso, A Venezuela en el centenario del libertador, quoted by Ruiz, Historia patria, p. 207.

complete shelving of such provisions of the constitution as were not in accord with his ever-changing interests and use of power, and his continuous projection before the nation of the image of his dominance and prowess.

He demanded absolute subordination of thought and action and resented any attempt on the part of his ministers to provide council and guidance pertaining to their own branch of administration. On one occasion he stated, "Those who serve me must break all ties and make them only with me, because I represent the Fatherland of today and of the future."

In the final years of his administration he built a palatial home in Antimano, some fifteen kilometers from Caracas, and since cabinet meetings were held every day he forced his ministers to go out there over a long, dusty road and severely castigated anyone who dared to be absent from any cabinet session. He would not even consider illness as a sufficient excuse, stating that: "Those who are working for me have no right to become ill." [3]

His attitude toward the military chiefs and the regional caudillos who were on several occasions responsible for returning him to power and keeping him in power was no less arbitrary. Disregarding the provisions of the constitution as to the sovereign rights of the states, he personally picked the state presidents and removed them at will. He suspiciously viewed the military chieftains as a possible threat to his power and often provoked situations which made it possible to eliminate them by death or by exile. He did not hesitate to resort to terror and the cunning manipulation or complete discard of those parts of the constitution that were not in accord with his ever-changing interests. This aspect of his regime is described elsewhere in this study. Here it suffices to quote a noteworthy statement of Guzmán Blanco's.

[3] *Ibid.*, p. 107.

Inasmuch as there often arose situations that were incompatible with the system of legal practices, my government had to be essentially authoritative. Because of this the policy was exclusively mine, born of me and imposed by me. Even the most courageous of my assistants found my policy excessively hard and cruel at times and, fearful of reprisals, they entreated me to moderate it. However, I maintained my determination to fight the war with fire and blood until I was either exterminated by the enemy or remained the complete victor on the vast battlefield of Venezuela.[4]

In this statement Guzmán Blanco acknowledges his use of autocratic methods and assumes full responsibility for his policy of oppression and reprisals. He admits that even his collaborators considered his methods hard and cruel and declares that he was primarily concerned about remaining the victor and, therefore, had no compunction about choosing the road of war and fire and blood.

Of particular importance during this stage was the inculcation of a sense of his supreme self-reliance and predominance into the nation and the masses. In his relations with his cabinet, the Liberal Party, and his associates he exhibited complete contempt for their views and opinions, rejected flatly ideas that he could not claim as his own, and was even anxious to be blamed for the indiscretions and transgressions of his subordinates to prove that all plans sprang from him alone, that no one could think for him or influence him, and that his was the first and final word. A striking example of this attitude was expressed in a letter to his father during the Rojas-Pereire protocol incident:

It is bad faith to attribute the project to Rojas—it is infamy and cowardice. He is being attacked because he does not have the power that I have and they are waiting to denounce me when I leave power as they did in 1877. No one in Venezuela should

4 Rondón Márquez, *Guzmán Blanco,* II, 103.

believe that any born person influences my plans. Everyone knows that I conceive everything in my head and do it with my own will without even discussing it with anybody. If there is anyone in the country who rejects the result of my great painstaking and patriotic efforts, I will, irrespective of what public opinion thinks, pay as little attention to him as I would to the expressions of the Indians of Guagira or of Caroní.[5]

Although stung by the criticism against the Rojas-Pereire protocol incident, he arrogantly assumed the authorship of the project and rejected any intimation that someone else had anything to do with conceiving or with carrying out this plan. He concludes that he intends to complete the project irrespective of the criticism or of the objections from the people.

In his relations with other people he brooked no opposition and would admit to no fallibility, as was shown in an anecdote related by Alirio Díaz Guerra.

On one occasion he wanted to extend a favor to a young man who was going to marry the daughter of one of his intimate associates. He summoned him and told him that he was going to name him an engineer in the ministry of public works. The young man told him that he was not an engineer. "How dare you!" shouted Guzmán Blanco imperiously. "You are an engineer. You have to be an engineer, and don't argue with me." "Yes, General, if you order so." "It is not what I order. It is what I do, and because of this you are going to take over the office of the director of the ministry of public works." [6]

And, Díaz Guerra concludes, the appointment was published in the official gazette the next day.[7]

A further development in this stage, perhaps natural in a caudillo who does not rest on hereditary rights, traditions, or

---

[5] Quoted by González Guinán, *Historia contemporánea de Venezuela*, XII, 134.

[6] *Diez años en Venezuela*, p. 101.

[7] *Ibid.*, p. 101.

a constitutional appointment and, therefore, feels the need
to bolster his self-importance, was Guzmán Blanco's growing
vanity and insatiable appetite for adulation.

A past master of flattery and fulsome adulation, as he had
proved himself to be in his association with Falcón, Guzmán
Blanco demanded and obtained the most tumultuous receptions and ovations, the highest degree of public acclaim, and
innumerable medals and decorations. A large number of
statues were erected in his honor in Caracas, La Guaira, and
other centers of the republic. Many states were named after
him and grandiloquent titles were attached to his name.

The parade of honors began in 1863 when, on June 30th,
the populace of societies of Caracas presented him with a
sword of honor. On April 21, 1864, the municipal congress of
Caracas gave him a gold medal commemorating the Treaty
of Coche. On December 31, 1872, the legislature of the state
of Bolívar adopted the name of Guzmán Blanco. On April
3, 1873, congress awarded to Guzmán Blanco the title of Illustrious American, Regenerator of Venezuela, and ordered
that an equestrian statue be erected in his honor with the
inscription, "To the Illustrious American, Regenerator of
Venezuela, General Antonio Guzmán Blanco, in National
Gratitude, 1873." On February 1, 1873, the legislature of the
state Guzmán Blanco decreed the erection of a statue of
Guzmán Blanco in the state capital, La Victoria.[8]

At the end of the Septenio, when General Alcántara was
already in office, Guzmán Blanco was given a special decora-
tion called the "Sun of April," awarded to him by congress in
commemoration of his entrance into Caracas on April 27,
1870. Again, when Guzmán Blanco returned after the Revolution of Revindication, the congress, by a decree issued on
October 28, 1879, ordered the reerection of the statues originally built in his honor in Caracas and other cities of the

---

[8] Hortensio, *Guzmán Blanco y su tiempo*, pp. 191 ff.

republic. To the unveiling of the statues in Caracas in 1879, there came the military chiefs, members of congress, representatives of military delegations and of municipal councils, and special commissions from all the states.

In the subsequent periods of his rule these manifestations of public adulation were no less numerous. In 1883, when the birthday of Bolívar was celebrated in Caracas, Guzmán Blanco used the event as an excuse for self-glorification to such an extent that it was not clear in whose honor the celebrations were being held, Bolívar's or Guzmán Blanco's. The celebrations were carried on under the slogan, "Viva Bolívar! Gloria a Guzmán!" ("Long live Bolívar! Glory to Guzmán!")

When we put forward these evidences of Guzmán Blanco's personalism as it is reflected in his employment of power, it may be objected that particular rulers of all kinds, even those whose authority was firmly grounded in a recognized legitimacy unpossessed by this caudillo, have exhibited similar tendencies to self-glorification. There were Roman emperors who proclaimed themselves gods and displayed inordinate vanity. There have been monarchs who demanded incessant adoration and regarded their subjects as no more than the means to gratify their whims, vanities, and lusts. There have been dictators of the charismatic type who were filled with overweening pride and wantonly abused their power so that it might serve their own aggrandizement. Why then should we peculiarly associate personalistic rule with a caudillo like Guzmán Blanco?

It is true that any ruler, especially an absolutist one, may show personalist tendencies in the sense that he comes to regard the function of government as the gratification of his personal wishes. "Power is poison," and its uncontrolled use destroys the recognition that it is a public trust. There remains, however, a difference between the full-blown personalism of Guzmán Blanco and the personalist tendencies generally to be found in rulers of another type. The absolute monarch may announce, *"L'état, c'est moi,"* but he is merely asserting in exaggerated form the old tradition, embodied in the formulas and rites of the royal prerogatives, that the country is the patrimony of the sovereign. The reverence attached to the person of the monarch, the divinity that "doth hedge a king," gave credence to the doctrine in the minds of many. Moreover, *Le Roi Soleil* did not claim this right by virtue of his personal achievement and merit but rather by virtue of his descent, his inheritance of office. His position, rooted in a tradition widely accepted, is totally unlike the the position of the lone caudillo who blusters his empty claim in a social vacuum and must magnify his own personality and his prowess in the attempt to buttress his position and to discourage the foes that always lie in wait to challenge his authority. The person of the monarch gains its transcendence from the majesty of his office, but the caudillo must artificially magnify his person in order to retain his office.

Take again the case of the charismatic dictator. He may be obsessed by the sense of his own greatness. He may be ruthless and arbitrary, but he represents himself as the mouthpiece of a cause, the agent of a great mission. He does not speak in his own name but in the name of the cause he embodies. He has the backing of the believers in the cause. He is not thrust back on his isolated personality. In the eyes of his followers, and usually of himself as well, the cause justifies him, enthrones him, determines the set direction of his policy.

Contrariwise, a caudillo such as Guzmán Blanco has no background to relieve his sheer insistence on his personal glory. There is no assurance behind his claims. He must assert his lone self because he has nothing else to assert. If he supports any cause it is merely from expediency. If he solemnly proclaims any principles as sacred to him, he is ready to sacrifice them whenever they cease to pay dividends to his power. It is not assurance but insecurity that animates his unbounded egoism. He must continually clutch at power. Always it threatens to slip through his fingers. He must impress other men with his glory. He must manufacture it for that purpose. He knows in his heart that his glory is only vainglory.

This cancer of vainglory grew in Guzmán Blanco and prepared the inevitable third stage in the career of a caudillo, the losing struggle to retain supremacy. Instead of establishing an assured order, Guzmán Blanco kept Venezuelan politics in a continuous turmoil. Instead of building his rule on solid loyalties, he achieved only the temporary adherence of self-interested parties and aroused forces that turned against him whenever he left power. The revolt of his own chosen candidate, General Alcántara, in 1878 and the complete rejection of his hegemony by President Rojas Paúl, whom he put in office over General Crespo, were direct results of the lack of solid loyalties and demonstrated the insecurity of personalism as a method of preserving political power.

Conclusion

Our study of venezuela and the case of Guzmán Blanco shows that one of the peculiarities of caudillismo, as a form of dictatorship, is that it occurs in avowedly democratic countries with supposedly democratic political machinery. It is seen how the constitution, the congress, the electorate— all patterned on democratic models—were used by Guzmán Blanco, not so much to attain the ends for which they were ostensibly designed but to attain his own ends. One of the most general conditions of caudillismo in Latin America would seem, therefore, to be the attempt to achieve democracy suddenly with a population ill-prepared for it and sharply divided within its own ranks.

The various countries emerged from a colonialism distinguished by its autocratic character. They were left with badly shattered economies as a result of the wars of independence and with relatively little by way of local political experience and tradition; and they were characterized by strong class and racial cleavages and by illiteracy and poverty. Yet, by virtue of the association of democracy with independence, as seen in the French Revolution and, above all, in the American Revolution and the formation of the United States of America, the new Latin American states generally sought to shape their governments along democratic lines. They drew up democratic constitutions, therefore, which incorporated the principles of democratic political organization. The idea of federalism, of a nation being a federation of local units having a maximum of autonomy, was in itself an extreme form of democratic thought—and one that had a certain plausibility in view of the role of the cabildos as the main form of local rule under the colonial regime and of the dispersion, local variation, and isolation in the society of the time. The result was a somewhat incongruous juxtaposition of highly elaborate political democracy, on the one hand, and a lack of social democracy and social preparedness on the other. In this situation—a situation vaguely analogous to that of the immigrant cities of the United States —the caudillo was almost the inevitable answer.

The caudillo is not an absolute ruler by any divine or human right—for such a right would be contrary to democracy. He is not a ruler by virtue of some new and powerful idea symbolized in his person and embodied in his actions— for that, too, is contrary to democracy and to the condition of a heterogeneous, scattered, and demoralized population. Rather, he is a ruler by virtue of political default, on the one hand, and personal ruthlessness and ingenuity on the other. The political default comes with the inability of the avowed political machinery to solve the problems of government in the situation of ignorance, poverty, dispersion, divisiveness, and lack of tradition characterizing the Latin American people after their emancipation from absolute colonialism. The fault does not lie in the democratic institutions themselves, but in the setting. The breakdown of government leaves a vacuum which no public can stand. Some semblance of order, some actual governing, is so necessary that it will be bought at any price. The price in this case is the caudillo, the strong man who is willing to use the existing political machinery to his own ends, to sacrifice his friends or placate his enemies as need be, and to secure himself by amassing a personal fortune at public expense. By virtue of the very manner through which he is selected, by virtue of the very process by which he emerges at the top, such a man cannot be governed by sincere belief in an ideology, genuine financial integrity, or strong personal attachment. He may have such ideas and sentiments, but he cannot let them govern his actions. Instead, these traits must be overridden by others —ideological irresponsibility, financial chicanery, and unqualified use of force. Other people follow the caudillo not so much because of his personal attractiveness as because of his being powerful. To continue in power he must at all costs maintain the practice of the characteristics which got him there in the first place. He must play friend against friend and enemy against enemy.

The price for political order obtained in this way is high. It does not generally lead to efficiency in government. On the other hand, it is better than no political order at all. Guzmán Blanco had somehow to govern, had to keep the nation going. He showed undeniable ability in governing. If he had not done this, he could not have accomplished what he did for himself privately. The caudillo thus gives some value received for the price paid.

Although dictatorship will doubtless be a frequent occurrence as long as human society lasts, caudillismo appears to be a temporary phenomenon. It will likely gradually disappear as the conditions that gave rise to it disappear. In different parts of Latin America and at different rates, social and economic modernization is taking place. Education, urbanization and industrialization, improved health and more international contact—these are all going ahead and showing signs of giving the sort of social milieu in which genuine democracy can provide an adequate government. In this new situation dictatorship may reappear from time to time, but the old-style caudillo seems on the wane.

The regime of Guzmán Blanco, when seen close-up and in detail, shows the danger of painting history solely in black and white. Although this man showed the characteristics of the caudillo to approximately an average degree, he also showed individual traits that distinguish him as a human being. His harsh qualities were combined with genuine ability. The exigencies of his career in the situation of the time in a sense forced the harsh qualities on him. They were the necessary characteristics of personal political survival. His excessive vanity, quite common among caudillos, was a result of, a sort of personal reward, the exercise of power. Appeals to his vanity symbolized and expressed for him and for others the fact that he had the power. It therefore contributes nothing to the understanding of caudillismo to blame the man who fills the role. If he had been a better man in the ethical sense, he could not have been a caudillo, but some other man would then have been the caudillo. Caudillismo is a product of social and political conditions prevailing in a certain time and place. It is not the product of good or bad traits in a particular individual. Nevertheless, a great deal is contributed to our understanding of caudillismo to see it in personal terms, in terms of a particular man who had a caudillo career. The present study has attempted to look at the phenomenon from this point of view. The success of the effort must be judged by the reader himself, but the value of the approach used seems beyond question.

BIBLIOGRAPHY

WORKS BY ANTONIO GUZMÁN BLANCO

Memorandum del General Guzmán Blanco. Caracas, 1875.

Mensajes presentados a los Congresos por el General Guzmán Blanco. Caracas, 1876.

La reivindicación: Documentos del General Guzmán Blanco. Caracas, 1879.

Discursos del General Guzmán Blanco. Caracas, 1883.

En defensa de la causa liberal. Paris, 1894.

Six articles written under the pen name "Alfa" in *El Federalista*. These are reprinted in Fausto Teodoro de Aldrey's *Rasgos biográficos*, pp. 201–270. Caracas, 1876.

OFFICIAL DOCUMENTS

Actos legislativos sancionados por el Congreso Nacional en 1874 y decretos ejecutivos dictados por el Presidente de la República General Guzmán Blanco hasta el 7 de junio del mismo año. Caracas, 1874.

A Letter Addressed to His Excellency, Don Antonio L. Guzmán by Messrs. Baring Brothers and Company. London, 1865. This publication also includes a collection of official documents in Spanish with English translations pertaining to the loan negotiations under the Páez dictatorship as well as the exchange of official correspondence by Guzmán Blanco, his father, and Baring Brothers.

Constitución del estado de Venezuela. Caracas, 1830.

Constitución de los Estados Unidos de Venezuela. Caracas, 1864.

Memoria de Hacienda: Exposición que a la Legislatura Nacional presenta el Ministro de Hacienda en 1865. Caracas, 1865.

Memoria de Hacienda: Exposición que a la Legislatura Nacional presenta el Ministro de Hacienda en 1866. Caracas, 1866.

Recopilación de leyes y decretos de Venezuela. Vols. I, II, III, IV, V, and VIII. Caracas, 1890.

GENERAL WORKS

Aldrey, Fausto Teodoro de, and Rafael Hernández Gutiérrez, eds. Rasgos biográficos. Caracas, 1876.

Alvarado, Lisandro. Historia de la revolución federal en Venezuela. Caracas, 1909.

Arcaya, Pedro Manuel. Estudios de sociología venezolana. Madrid, 1916.

―――― The Gómez Régime in Venezuela and Its Background. Washington, D. C., 1936.

―――― Influencia del elemento venezolano en la independencia de la América Latina. Caracas, 1916.

Arciniegas, Germán. America—Terra Firme. Santiago, 1937.

Arévalo González, R. Apuntaciones históricas. Caracas, 1913.

Arguedas, Alcides. Pueblo enfermo: Contribución a la psicología de los pueblos hispano americanos. Barcelona, 1910.

―――― Los caudillos bárbaros. Barcelona, 1929.

Ayarragaray, Lucas. La anarquía argentina y el caudillismo. Buenos Aires, 1904.

Baralt, Rafael María. Resumen de la historia de Venezuela. 3 vols. Paris, 1939.

Bigotte, Felix E. El libro de oro. Privately Printed, Caracas, 1866.

Blanco Fombona, Rufino. La evolución política y social de Hispano América. Madrid, 1911.

Briceño, Manuel. Los ilustres. Bogotá, 1884.

Carrancá y Trujillo, Raúl. La evolución política de Iberoamérica. Madrid, 1925.

Carreño, Eduardo. Vida anecdótica de venezolanos. Caracas, 1948.

Cecil, Jane. Libertad y despotismo en la América Hispánica. Madrid, 1931.

Chapman, Charles E. A History of the Cuban Republic: A Study in Hispanic American Politics. New York, 1927.

―――― "The Age of the Caudillos: A Chapter in Hispanic-American History," Hispanic American Historical Review, XII, August, 1932, pp. 281–300.

―――― Colonial Hispanic America: A History. New York, 1933.

Cova, J. A. Geografía física, política y económica de Venezuela. Caracas, 1945.

Dávila, Vicente. Investigaciones históricas. 2 vols. Caracas, 1923–27.

Díaz Guerra, Alirio. Diez años en Venezuela. Caracas, 1933.

Eastwick, Edward B. Sketches of Life in a South American Republic with the History of the Loan of 1864. London, 1868.

Gallegos, Manuel Modesto. Anales contemporáneos. Caracas, 1925.

García Calderón, Francisco. Latin America, Its Rise and Progress. Translated by Bernard Miall. London, 1913.

Gil Fortoul, José. Historia constitucional de Venezuela. 3 vols. Caracas, 1942.

González Guinán, Francisco. Historia contemporánea de Venezuela. 14 vols. Caracas, 1924.

Guzmán, Antonio Leocadio. Editoriales de El Venezolano. Caracas, 1883.

Hortensio. Guzmán Blanco y su tiempo. Caracas, 1883.

Humboldt, Alexander von. Voyage aux régions équinoxiales du nouveau continent. 24 vols. Paris, 1805–34.

Humphreys, R. A. The Evolution of Modern Latin America. New York, 1946.

James, Preston E. Latin America. New York, 1942.

Level de Goda, Luis. Historia contemporánea de Venezuela política y militar. Barcelona, 1893.

MacIver, R. M. The Web of Government. New York, 1947.

Matos, M. A. Recuerdos. Caracas, 1927.

Mecham, J. Lloyd. Church and State in Latin America. Chapel Hill, 1934.

Mijares, Augusto. La interpretación pesimista de la sociología hispana americana. Caracas, 1938.

Mollien, Gaspard Théodore. Viaje por la república de Colombia en 1823. Bogotá, 1944.

Moore, David. A History of Latin America. New York, 1945.

Moses, Bernard. The Establishment of Spanish Rule in America. New York, 1898.

—— The Spanish Dependencies in South America. 2 vols. London, 1914.

—— Spain's Declining Power in South America, 1730–1806. Berkeley, 1919.

—— South America on the Eve of Emancipation. New York, 1916.

—— Spanish Colonial Literature in South America. New York, 1922.

Ospina Londoño, Jorge. Pascual Bravo: Los partidos políticos en Colombia. Medellín, 1938.

Pachano, Jacinto R. Biografía del Mariscal Juan C. Falcón. Paris, 1876.

Páez, José Antonio. Autobiografía. New York, 1867.

Perera, Ambrosio. Historia orgánica de Venezuela. Caracas, 1943.

Picón-Febres, Gonzalo. La literatura venezolana en el siglo diez y nueve. Buenos Aires, 1947.

—— Nacimiento de Venezuela intelectual. Caracas, 1939.

Picón Salas, Mariano. De la conquista a la independencia. Mexico, 1944.

Pierson, W. W., ed. Studies in Hispanic-American History. Chapel Hill, 1927.

Ponce de León, Salvador. Análisis crítico de las dictaduras. Universidad Nacional de México, 1935.

Pons, François Raymond Joseph de. Voyage à la partie orientale de la Terre-firme dans l'Amérique méridionale. Paris, 1806.

Ramos, Arturo. Las culturas negras en el nuevo mundo. Mexico, 1943.

Reyes, Antonio. Primeras damas de Venezuela en el siglo XIX. Caracas, 1948.

Rippy, James Fred. Historical Evolution of Hispanic America. New York, 1944.

—— "Dictatorship in Latin America," Dictatorship in the Modern World, ed. by C. S. Ford. Minneapolis, 1939.

Robertson, William Spence. History of the Latin American Nations. 3d ed. New York, 1943.

Rodríguez Villa, Antonio. El teniente general Don Pablo Morillo, primer conde de Cartagena. 4 vols. Madrid, 1908–10.

Rojas Arístides. Humboldtianas. Caracas, 1942.

Rondón Márquez, Rafael. Guzmán Blanco. 2 vols. Caracas, 1944.

Roscher, Wilhelm. The Spanish Colonial System. Translation, ed. by E. G. Bourne. New York, 1904.

Ruiz, Luis (pseudonym of Domingo A. Olavarría). Historia patria. Valencia, 1895.

Simpson, Leslie Byrd. Many Mexicos. New York, 1941.

Solórzano de Pereira, Juan de. Política indiana. 2 vols. Madrid, 1736–39.

Soto, César Humberto. Personajes célebres de Venezuela. Caracas, 1948.

Tannenbaum, Frank. The Mexican Agrarian Revolution. New York, 1929.

——— Peace by Revolution: An Interpretation of Mexico. New York, 1933.

——— Whither Latin America? New York, 1934.

——— Slave and Citizen. New York, 1947.

Uslar Pietri, Arturo. Sumario de economía venezolana. Caracas, 1945.

Vallenilla Lanz, Laureano. Cesarismo democrático. Caracas, 1929.

——— Disgregación e integración. Caracas, 1930.

Vargas Vila, J. M. Los divinos y los humanos. Paris, 1903.

——— Los Césares de la decadencia. Barcelona, 1936.

Venturino, Agustín. Sociología general americana. Barcelona, 1931.

Villanueva, Laureano. Vida del valiente ciudadano General Ezequiel Zamora. Caracas, 1898.

Watters, Mary. A History of the Church in Venezuela, 1810–1930. Chapel Hill, 1933.

Weber, Max. Wirtschaft und Gesellschaft. Tübingen, 1925.

Whitbeck, R. H. Economic Geography of South America. Rev. ed. by F. E. Williams and W. F. Christians. New York, 1940.

Wilgus, A. Curtis, ed. Argentina, Brazil, and Chile since Independence. Washington, D. C., 1935.

——— ed. South American Dictators During the First Century of Independence. Washington, D. C., 1937.

Williams, Mary Wilhelmine. "The Political Problems of Hispanic

America: Their Origin and Nature," *South Atlantic Quarterly*, XXI, January, 1922.

────── The People and Politics of Latin America. Rev. ed., New York, 1945.

INDEX

Monagas, Ruperto, 74, 116

Monies, decree on, 88

Morgan, W., Company, 154

Morillo, Pablo, quoted, 21

Morning Chronicle, The, 150 f.

Morny, Duke of, 103, 105; contract for piping the aqueduct of Macarao, 160

Nadal, Hilarion, 146

Negroes: importation into Venezuela, 6 f.; social conditions, 8

Newspaper editors, imprisonment of, 104

North American Company, 105

Oduber, Luis, 155; contract for lighthouse, 156

Oligarchy, affluent classes favored under, 38

Opinión Nacional, La, 102, 124, 140, 144

Opportunism, characteristic of Guzmán Blanco's regime, 112

Otazo, Abdon, 138, 143

Pachano, Jacinto, 114, 152 f.

Páez, José Antonio, 35, 41; creoles allied with, 37; his support sought by Guzmán, 44; break with Monagas, 46

Parades of honor, 170

Pardo, Francisco G., "Power of the Idea," 140

Pardos, Royal Decree of April 14, 1795, concerning, 8 ff.

Paúl, Rojas, 105; election to the presidency, 106; hostility toward Guzmán Blanco, 108–9; election to the presidency, 132; break with Guzmán Blanco, 133; relations with Guzmán Blanco, 160

Pereire, Eugenio Rodríguez, 158 f.

Pérez, Juan Francisco: contracts for public works given to, 155; contracts a steamship and a telegraph line, 156

Pérez, Salomé, 138

Personalism, 161 ff.; difference between that of Guzmán Blanco and other absolute monarchs, 171 f.; insecurity of, 172 f.

Philip II, 4

Philip V, control of the Guipuzcoana Company, 29

Pile, W. A., 159

Píritu, granted to the Franciscan Observants, 4

Pius IX, liberalism condemned by, 85

Ponte, José Antonio, 121, 128 f., 129

President, tenure of office, 38

Press, the, repressive measures against, 139 ff.

Prisoners: liberation of, 86, 88; Guzmán Blanco's attitude toward, 136

Provinces, 15 ff.

Puerto Cabello: campaign against, 81 f.; Guzmán Blanco's efforts to control the import duties of, 148

Pulido, Ignacio, 117, 125; insurrection of Coro incited by, 92; Guzmán Blanco's defeat of, 141

Quinquenio, the, 98 ff.

Quintero, José Angel: dismissal of Guzmán, 41; propaganda campaign against Monagas, 46

Races, 1 ff.; mixture of, 12 ff.

Railroads: between Puerto Cabello and Valencia, 99; contracts for, 157; foreign financing of, 160

Rangel, Francisco José, 45

Rational legitimacy, *see* Legitimacy

Reducción system, 3

Reinvindicadores, 95

Repartimientos, 3

Reprisals, Guzmán Blanco's policy of, 168

Resquardos, 4

Revolutionary attempts, 143 f.

Revolution of 1879, 130

Rojas, José María: negotiator of large contracts, 155; contract for a steamship line, 156; negotiations with Pereire, 158 f.; contract with General Pérez made by, 156